I0624061

Journey To Redemption

Finding Freedom in the Chaos

D.R Young

Published by Hemingway Publishers

Cover design by Hemingway Publishers

ISBN: Printed in the United States

HEMINGWAY
PUBLISHERS

Dedication

"In our journey, some people change your life and bring hope, joy, and laughter. For me, that has been my two sons and daughter-in-law. I dedicate this book to them! Samuel, Matthew, and Joelle."

Endorsements

"Pastor Deano Young has been a close personal friend for over 30 years since our Bible school days. In this book, Deano speaks directly from God's Word and his personal experience in dealing with life's tragedies through faith, trust, and perseverance. It is a wonderful tool to help every believer in their spiritual growth and development."

Pastor Jeffery White
Lead Pastor, Prolific Communicator
Emmanuel Pentecostal Church
Deer Lake NL

"Each of us is on a journey we call life experience. It can be enjoyable and challenging. In this his first book, the author and my good friend, Deano Young shares a wealth of information to help you and me navigate the journey. Sharing from scripture, his own experience and testimonies of fellow travelers who are navigating life by researching the writings of others, Deano provides tools and methods for overcoming the journey, no matter what obstacle life brings. Journey to Redemption can serve as a helpful guide in overcoming, prevailing in the storm, and finding hope, wholeness, and healing in one's life experience. I believe it will help you and others find hope for the rest of the journey."

Pastor William Harnum
Retired Pastor, PAONL

"It is without hesitation that I recommend Deano's book, 'Journey to Redemption' to anyone who is seeking to strengthen their faith and their walk with God. Having known Deano for the past 20 years, we can see how his book is a result and culmination of many years of faithfully serving God and His church. You can hear in these pages the heart of a man who genuinely loves the Word of God and has a passion for discipleship! It has been a privilege for my wife and I to have known Deano and listen to his Spirit-filled and anointed messages. The wisdom in his book will inspire and guide you, as you face the challenges and storms in your life! May you be blessed as you read this book."

Kenneth Doucet
RSW, Mental Health Therapist
Red Deer, AB

"In reading this book Dr Deano Young will help you navigate between the faith one needs and the storms of life which create the faith to propel you into the plan that God has for your life. Every situation requires an element of Faith. In this book Dr Deano challenges us to dig down to the deep depths of our soul and get to where we must put our total trust in God. Are you lonely? Are you confused? Do you not know how to navigate the challenges of life? Dr Deano Young will help you know that God has not given up on you. No matter what the situation. There is redemption, there is restoration there is a place where you can ask God to help you navigate your journey. This book will give you practical steps that will help you trust God and people again and others who may walk with you through some of the storms of life. You are not alone. God is with you. May your faith be strengthened.

Bishop Dr. Greg Gill

Ever Increasing Ministries
Calgary, AB Canada

About the Author

D. R Young was born and raised on the east coast of Canada. He now lives in the province of Alberta, Canada. He is the proud dad of two adult children and one daughter-in-law. He is an ordained pastor and is currently completing his Doctorate in Ministry. He has a master's degree in pastoral Counseling and has been given an honorary Doctor of Pastoral Counselling. He is the dean of the Canadian Christian Theological Seminary and serves on the board of the Evangelical Order of Certified Pastoral Counselors of America. He holds a membership with the American Association of Christian Counselors.

CONTENTS

Page Blank Intentionally

Introduction

In a world that keeps moving faster and faster, many people find themselves searching for something to hold on to. We live among constant updates, new technologies, and social pressures that make life overwhelming. This sense of chaos is especially true for teens and adults trying to understand their freedom through Christ. They often struggle with balancing personal freedoms and social responsibilities, leading to confusion about their beliefs.

Amid this confusion, strengthening one's faith becomes incredibly important. Faith isn't just a religious idea; it's a practical tool for dealing with life's challenges. Think of faith as an anchor that helps you stay grounded when everything else seems shaky. It gives you a stable foundation to face personal, social, or even economic obstacles. For example, consider the story of Joseph from Genesis. Despite being sold into slavery and facing numerous hardships, Joseph's unwavering faith in God's plan led him to save his family and many others from famine. His journey shows how strong faith can guide us through tough times and lead to unexpected good outcomes. In this chapter, we'll explore why strengthening your faith matters a lot today. We'll look at how faith and reason can work together, offering insights to help you navigate modern life's complexities. We'll dive into stories and practical steps rooted in biblical wisdom that can turn abstract beliefs into real-life actions. By the end of this chapter, you'll have a clearer understanding of how to build a resilient faith that supports you through any storm. Get ready to see how faith can be a comforting refuge and a powerful catalyst for change.

Relevance and Significance

In today's fast-paced world, filled with uncertainties and trials, many individuals seek guidance and solace in their faith. The constant flow of information, rapid technological advancements, and societal pressures can overwhelm anyone. This is particularly true for adults and teens struggling to understand their freedom through Christ. They are navigating a landscape where individual liberties and social responsibilities often clash, leading to confusion and questioning of long-held beliefs.

Strengthening one's faith is not merely a religious exercise but a lifeline amid such chaos. It's about finding an anchor, a sense of stability that allows individuals to weather life's storms with resilience and hope. Faith provides a foundation upon which we can build our responses to the challenges we face, whether they are personal, social, or economic.

In a world where empirical evidence and data often drive decisions, it's crucial to recognize that faith and reason are not mutually exclusive. On the contrary, they complement each other beautifully. Strengthening faith amidst the noise requires practical insights and wisdom from various aspects of life, including biblical teachings. This book aims to offer such insights, helping readers navigate their paths with both heart and mind engaged.

One of the primary struggles individuals face in strengthening their faith is the pervasive sense of isolation. It's easy to feel alone when challenges arise, as if no one understands what you're going through. However, faith teaches us that we are never truly alone. A higher power always guides us, and a community of believers supports us. This shared experience can be a powerful source of comfort and strength.

For instance, consider the story of Joseph in Genesis. Sold into slavery by his brothers, Joseph's journey was fraught with hardship and betrayal. Yet, through unwavering faith and trust in God's plan, he rose to a position of incredible influence, ultimately saving his family and many others from famine (Ingram, C., 2021). His story serves as a poignant reminder that faith can lead to unexpected and transformative outcomes even in the darkest times.

Moreover, the importance of applying practical steps in living out one's faith can't be overstated. Practical insights grounded in biblical wisdom can help transform theoretical knowledge into actionable life changes. By integrating these principles into daily life, individuals can cultivate an unwavering faith that withstands any storm.

One key step in this process is reverencing God's ways. Reverence involves respect and a deep-seated commitment to align one's actions and decisions with divine will. It's about recognizing that God's wisdom often surpasses human understanding and choosing to follow His guidance even when it seems counterintuitive.

Another critical aspect is understanding His word. This means diving deep into Scripture, not just skimming through it. It's about being students of the Word, meditating on its teachings, and seeking to apply them in everyday situations. Understanding Scripture brings clarity and insight, enabling individuals to make wise decisions and act with integrity.

Furthermore, asking for God's wisdom plays a pivotal role. According to James 1:5, "If any of you lacks wisdom, you should ask God, who gives generously to all without finding fault," and it will be given to you.

This promise underscores the accessibility of divine wisdom. God's generosity ensures that anyone who seeks wisdom with sincerity and faith will receive it, guiding in making tough decisions, managing relationships, and navigating life's complexities.

Lastly, learning to trust Him completely is essential. Trust goes beyond mere acceptance; it involves deep confidence in God's plan, regardless of the visible circumstances. It's about believing that God's decisions, decrees, and will are orchestrated for the highest good, even when we can't comprehend the bigger picture. This level of trust requires patience and perseverance, but it ultimately leads to a more profound and resilient faith.

By embracing these principles, individuals can find strength and peace in their faith, enabling them to face life's uncertainties with confidence and grace. Faith becomes a source of empowerment, allowing them to transcend fear and embrace a sense of purpose and direction.

In conclusion, this book offers a blend of practical insights and biblical wisdom designed to help readers strengthen their faith. It addresses the struggles and challenges of modern life, providing tools and strategies to cultivate an unwavering faith. As we navigate the complexities of today's world, let us remember that faith is not just a refuge but also a powerful catalyst for personal and collective growth.

Embracing faith with an open heart and mind can lead to transformative experiences, enriching our lives and those around us.

Preview of the Transformative Journey

In today's polarized world, strengthening faith has never been more crucial. As you embark on this journey, you'll discover how each chapter focuses on different ways to fortify your faith, helping you navigate life's storms with confidence and grace.

This transformative journey begins by understanding the unique challenges we face. Each of us encounters various obstacles that test our beliefs. Through stories, data, and practical insights, we will explore how these challenges can be met with resilience and faith. Next, we'll delve into methods for strengthening your faith, providing tools and practices rooted in personal experience and empirical evidence. These techniques help you grow spiritually and emotionally, enhancing your capacity to trust and believe even in difficult times.

Fear is a natural part of life but doesn't have to control or define you. In one of the chapters, we'll look closely at how fear manifests and offer strategies to overcome it effectively.

Dr. Schubiner states fear often stems from early experiences and learned behaviors (Dr. Schubiner -Understanding and Overcoming Fear. TMS Forum (The Mindbody Syndrome)., n.d.).

Understanding the source of your fears can empower you to face them head-on. Here are some things you can do to manage fear:

- Recognize fear as a universal emotion. Accepting its presence can reduce its power over you.
- Identify what specifically is causing your fear. Is it a past event, future, or immediate concern?
- Understand what fear is trying to teach you. Often, it's a signal from your mind to protect yourself from perceived danger.
- Face your fears directly. Doing so can diminish their hold on you over time.
- Use meditation techniques to calm your mind and separate yourself from the intensity of fearful emotions.
- Apply reasoning skills to challenge the messages of fear. Remind yourself that fear's predictions are often incorrect.
- Express your fears through writing or speaking. This can help you process and understand them better.
- Take action against situations causing fear when possible. Confronting these issues head-on can reduce their impact.
- Cultivate gratitude and act with purpose. Positive actions can mitigate feelings of fear and anxiety.

Another chapter will guide you toward embracing peace. Peace isn't just about the absence of conflict but also the presence of tranquility and assurance. We'll examine how cultivating inner peace can transform your outlook and interactions with others. By practicing mindfulness and focusing on the present moment, you can develop a more peaceful state of mind.

Prayer is a powerful tool that connects us to a higher purpose. In a dedicated chapter, we'll explore how harnessing the power of prayer can bring about profound changes in your life. Prayer isn't just about asking for help; it's also about expressing gratitude, seeking guidance, and finding comfort. By incorporating regular prayer into your routine, you can strengthen your spiritual connection and reinforce your faith.

Throughout the book, real-life stories and testimonials will illustrate the principles discussed, making the concepts more relatable and easier to apply. Challenges like health care, housing, and education have shown us the need for balanced solutions considering economic growth and human welfare. In advocating for reforms, we must hand more power to individuals while ensuring a safety net for those who fall on hard times. Personal responsibility and social support create a robust framework for dealing with life's uncertainties.

Understanding that everyone faces struggles and setbacks is key to empathy and compassion. As you read through each chapter, you'll learn to apply these lessons in your own life and become a source of support for others. The more we share our journeys and insights, the stronger our collective faith becomes.

This transformative journey is about individual growth and

building a community of like-minded people who support and uplift each other. By sharing your experiences, engaging in discussions, and applying what you've learned, you contribute to a larger movement towards living victoriously and celebrating the power of faith. Together, we can create a world where faith thrives despite challenges, and everyone feels empowered to face their fears and embrace peace.

So, prepare to dive deep, reflect, and take actionable steps. Each chapter builds upon the last, guiding you toward a life filled with unwavering faith, inner peace, and the joy that comes from living in alignment with your values. This book is your companion on this journey, offering wisdom, encouragement, and practical advice every step of the way.

Engaging the Reader

In this chapter, we've delved deeply into the importance of faith in today's fast-paced and often overwhelming world. We've seen how strengthening faith isn't just a religious act but a vital source of stability and hope. Life throws countless challenges our way, from personal struggles to societal pressures, making us question long-held beliefs. But faith anchors us, offering a foundation to navigate through these storms.

Earlier, we touched on how faith and reason aren't at odds but complement each other. This balance helps us understand that nurturing faith requires both heart and mind. Embracing practicality alongside spiritual wisdom allows us to grow grounded and meaningfully.

So, where are we now? We've explored that feeling isolated during tough times is a common struggle. Yet, faith teaches us that we are never truly alone. The story of Joseph, who overcame betrayal and hardship through unwavering faith, serves as an inspiring example. This shows us that faith can lead to incredible outcomes even in the darkest moments.

For some readers, the journey to strengthen faith may seem daunting. You might worry about feeling isolated or not knowing how to apply what you've learned. These concerns are valid, but remember, the tools and insights shared here are designed to help you integrate faith into your daily life. Whether practicing reverence, diving deep into Scripture, asking for God's wisdom, or learning to trust Him completely, each step brings you closer to a resilient and unshakeable faith.

On a broader scale, imagine a world where more people embrace their faith amidst life's challenges. Communities would be stronger, support systems more robust, and individuals more equipped to handle adversity gracefully. Faith doesn't just benefit us personally; it has the potential to create ripples of positive change around us.

As we wrap up this chapter, consider how these principles can be a catalyst for personal and collective growth. What steps will you take to strengthen your faith today? How will your actions influence those around you? Reflecting on these questions can guide you as you continue this transformative journey. Let's move forward with an open heart and mind, ready to embrace the power of faith in every aspect of our lives.

Chapter One.

Understanding Life's Storms

L ife's storms are like the unexpected thunderstorms that pop up on a sunny afternoon. There's no avoiding them, and they often come without warning. These challenges can leave us feeling shaken and unsure of our footing. But what if we saw these storms as opportunities instead of obstacles? What if we viewed each one through the lens of faith, seeing God's hand at work even in our toughest moments? This chapter dives into this transformative perspective, urging us to find meaning and growth in life's inevitable hardships.

Take a closer look at some of the Bible's most profound stories for guidance on navigating these storms. Job's story is a powerful example; despite his immense suffering, he never lost his faith in God. He questioned and lamented but stayed firm in his belief. This unwavering faith eventually led to restoration and blessings beyond measure. Another tale is that of Joseph, who endured betrayal and slavery yet rose to a position of great power, showing us that perseverance through adversity can lead to the fulfillment of God's promises. Then there's Paul, who faced persecution, imprisonment, and shipwrecks yet remained steadfast in spreading the gospel. His endurance is a beacon of faithfulness, showcasing how challenges can fortify our resolve and deepen our trust in God's plan.

This chapter will explore the nature and purpose of life's storms through a biblical lens. We'll delve into how these trials can transform our character and strengthen our faith. You'll discover practical steps to face these challenges with courage and resilience, such as seeking spiritual growth, relying on prayer, and finding strength in the community. By understanding the divine purpose behind our struggles, we can learn to embrace them as opportunities to grow closer to God and become stronger versions of ourselves.

Storms Will Come, and they can be transformative.

Like the changing seasons, life's storms are an inevitable part of the human experience. These trials and challenges are not designed to destroy us but to strengthen and refine our character. God uses these storms to mold us into better versions of ourselves. By looking at biblical examples, we can find valuable lessons to apply in our own lives.

Job, for instance, faced unimaginable loss and suffering yet held on to his faith. He questioned, he lamented, but he never abandoned his trust in God. His story shows us that even when everything appears bleak, maintaining faith can bring restoration and blessings beyond measure (THE PATIENCE OF JOSEPH. pacificcog.org., n.d.). Then there's Joseph, whose journey from being sold into slavery by his brothers to rising as a powerful leader in Egypt demonstrates how perseverance through adversity eventually leads to the fulfillment of God's promises (THE PATIENCE OF JOSEPH. pacificcog.org., n.d.).

Paul's endurance of persecution and hardship while spreading the gospel is another beacon of unwavering faith. Despite beatings, imprisonment, and shipwrecks, Paul remained steadfast, driven by his conviction and love for Christ. Through these narratives, it's clear we've got essential guidance for navigating our life's storms.

When we understand God's purpose in allowing these trials, it becomes easier to face them with courage. Challenges serve as tools for growth and spiritual maturity and deepen our reliance on God's providence. By viewing our struggles as opportunities for personal and spiritual growth, we recognize that God works all things together for the good of those who love Him

To make the most out of these challenging times, here's what you can do:

- Look for opportunities to grow spiritually.

- Use prayer and scripture study to build your faith reservoir.
- Focus on serving others to gain perspective on your own trials.
- Reflect on past experiences where you saw God's hand at work.

Storms are indeed catalysts for transformation. They lead to greater resilience and trust in God's providence. When we face adversity, we often discover new facets of our faith and deepen our relationship with God. Here's what you can do to recognize this growth potential:

- Keep a journal of your experiences and how they shape your faith.
- Engage in honest conversations with God about your struggles.
- Seek fellowship with others who share your faith journey.

We open the door to profound spiritual insights by fully embracing these growth opportunities. The process isn't just about enduring; it's about thriving and evolving into stronger, more resilient individuals grounded in faith.

In summary, while life's storms can be daunting, they offer extraordinary opportunities for growth and deeper divine connection. Through unwavering faith and trust in God's plan, we emerge from these trials stronger and with a renewed sense of purpose and closer intimacy with God. Remember, every storm you weather is a step toward becoming the person God intends you to be. So, equip yourself with faith, lean on scriptural wisdom, and recognize each challenge as an opportunity for transformative growth.

Trials and spiritual refinement.

The refining fire of trials is an essential concept that traces its roots back to the natural refinement process. Imagine gold taken from the earth, riddled with impurities and barely recognizable for its worth. To reveal its true value, the gold must pass through intense flames that melt away the dross, leaving only the pure metal. Similarly, life's challenges act as a refining fire for our faith and character. Just as the heat purifies gold, trials we endure purify us, revealing the essence of who we are and what we can become.

Embracing this process leads to a deeper understanding of God's sovereignty and provision. When faced with difficulties, it's helpful to remember that these moments are not random acts devoid of purpose. Instead, they are carefully placed experiences meant to shape and refine us. Here is what you can do in order to achieve this understanding:

- First, acknowledge that trials are part of God's plan.
- Second, remind yourself that God is in control.
- Third, trust in His wisdom and timing.

16

- Fourth, seek to find the lessons within the struggle.

By doing so, the refining fire becomes less about the pain and more about the growth it encourages.

Now, let's talk about the role of perseverance in spiritual maturation. Perseverance, the steadfastness in doing something despite difficulty or delay, is crucial in deepening our faith. This endurance fosters patience and an unwavering trust in God's faithfulness. Our resilience grows as we persevere through various storms, fortifying the foundation upon which our faith stands.

Consider how perseverance cultivated during challenging times gives birth to a robust spiritual maturity. The journey through life's hardships isn't merely about reaching the other side; it's about who we become during the journey. As we navigate these storms, our character is tested, our faith is solidified, and we learn to lean on God's promises even more heavily.

Encouraging readers to view challenges as opportunities for growth rather than insurmountable obstacles shifts the narrative from despair to hope. Each trial encountered is a step closer to a profound spiritual insight and personal evolution. The transformative nature of these trials paves the way for a stronger connection with God and a reliance on His grace. Here is what you can do:

- First, change your perspective on challenges.

- Second, look at each difficulty as a chance to grow.
- Third, embrace the lessons learned during tough times.
- Fourth, rely on God's grace throughout the process.

This approach transforms adversity into a powerful catalyst for spiritual enrichment.

Recognizing the beauty that emerges from undergoing trials brings a new appreciation for the refining process. Through God's work in our lives, we are molded into vessels of grace, reflecting His light to those around us. The significance lies not in avoiding brokenness but in finding beauty through restoration. Recognizing the beauty in brokenness enhances our appreciation for the journey through life's storms. Such awareness fosters a sense of gratitude and fortitude, knowing that each trial has a purpose in the grand tapestry of our lives.

As we walk through life's challenges, we must understand that our trials and tribulations serve as opportunities for remarkable transformation. The refining fire, though painful, is never without reason. It burns away our impurities, shapes our character, and draws us closer to God. By embracing this process, we allow ourselves to be more deeply connected to God, leaning on His everlasting provision and mercy.

In conclusion, viewing life's trials through a biblical lens provides solace and a profound sense of purpose. Embrace the refining fire of trials as it purifies your faith and character. Recognize the role of perseverance in fostering spiritual maturity and see challenges as opportunities for growth. Finally, appreciate the beauty that comes from walking through the fire and emerging stronger and more refined on the other side. Through this journey, may you find a deeper relationship with God and an unshakeable trust in His divine craftsmanship.

Spiritual and transformative potential in life's storms.

A divine perspective on challenges:

When life throws challenges at us, it's easy to feel overwhelmed and disheartened. However, adopting a divine perspective can transform these trials into opportunities for growth. Instead of seeing difficulties as insurmountable obstacles, try viewing them as divine assignments. Here's how you can shift your perspective:

- First, invite God into your situation by asking for His wisdom and guidance through prayers.
- Second, look for lessons that God might be teaching you in the midst of your struggles.
- Third, keep your heart open to the possibility that these challenges are preparing you for future blessings or tasks.

This shift from despair to hope brings comfort and deepens our understanding of God's purpose. Embracing these divine assignments fosters a sense of purpose and resilience, equipping us to face adversity with newfound strength.

The transformative power of faith:

Faith acts as a guiding light in times of hardship, leading us through the darkest moments. By cultivating and strengthening our faith, we bolster our ability to withstand any storm with unwavering confidence. Faith inspires courage, perseverance, and trust in God's promises, making it an invaluable ally in overcoming life's challenges.

Discovering hidden blessings in trials:

Life's storms often carry hidden blessings within them. When faced with adversity, we have the chance to develop resilience, character, and spiritual insight. God's grace abounds even in turmoil, providing comfort, wisdom, and strength. Here's how to uncover these hidden blessings:

- Reflect on past challenges and identify the ways they have shaped you positively.
- Stay alert for new opportunities that arise as a result of overcoming difficulties.
- Trust that God's grace is at work, even when outcomes are not immediately clear.

Recognizing and embracing these hidden blessings teaches us that trials can lead to profound personal and spiritual growth.

Embracing the journey of transformation:

Life's storms can be incredibly challenging, yet they offer unique opportunities for transformation. When we trust in God's redemptive power, these hardships become part of a larger, divine refinement process.

Embracing this journey involves:

- Accepting that every trial has a purpose in God's grand design.
- Seeing each challenge as a step towards deeper faith and spiritual maturity.
- Trusting that God's sovereignty and provision will see you through every circumstance.

Through faith and perseverance, we emerge from trials not as victims but as victors, empowered by our unwavering trust in God's goodness. This refined perspective allows us to appreciate the depth of God's love and provision, even in the most difficult times.

Key takeaways:

Understanding challenges from a divine perspective helps us harness faith's transformative power. It enables us to discover hidden blessings in adversity and embrace the journey of spiritual growth amid life's storms. By trusting in God's purpose, cultivating resilience, and seeking the lessons in our trials, we can navigate through life with peace and purpose.

Growth and resilience developed through life's storms.

A testament to resilience and faith: It's easy to feel overwhelmed in moments of adversity. Yet, the stories of those who have faced life's storms with unshakable faith remind us of the power within. Take Emily, for example—a woman who battled cancer not once but twice. Through her journey, she relied on prayer. She found comfort in Scripture, particularly in Psalms 46:1, which states, "God is our refuge and strength, an ever-present help in trouble." Her story serves as a beacon of hope, emphasizing that faith can be our guiding light even in our darkest moments.

Testimonies like Emily's are powerful because they illustrate how faith can turn obstacles into opportunities for growth. If you're facing your own challenges, here are some steps you can take:

- Reflect on inspiring testimonies of others who have overcome similar difficulties.
- Surround yourself with supportive communities that reinforce your faith.
- Lean into daily practices such as prayer, reading Scripture,

or journaling to maintain spiritual strength.

Lessons in perseverance and trust: Examining the stories of individuals who have triumphed over tribulation offers insights into enduring faith. John, a father who lost his job during an economic downturn, had every reason to despair. But he chose instead to trust in God's plan, reflecting on Proverbs 3:5-6, "Trust in the Lord with all your heart and lean not on your own understanding; in all your ways submit to him, and he will make your paths straight." This kind of trust doesn't come easily but grows through repeated acts of faith.

To build this kind of perseverance and trust in your own life:

- Regularly reflect on scriptures that emphasize trust in God.
- Keep a journal of personal trials and how faith has helped you navigate them.
- Engage in group discussions or Bible studies focused on trust and perseverance.

By examining these narratives, readers gain practical insights into maintaining faith during tough times. These lessons, drawn from real-life experiences, can strengthen your resolve and deepen your reliance on God's providence.

The beauty of a tested faith: Faith tested by fire reveals its true beauty. The glow of a diamond only comes after being subjected to intense pressure. Similarly, individuals who emerge stronger from their trials radiate a profound inner light. Consider

Sarah, who faced years of infertility but found solace in praying and meditating on Romans 8:28, "And we know that in all things God works for the good of those who love him." Her faith didn't just survive the trial - it flourished, inspiring others around her.

Witnessing such faith can inspire hope and fortitude in readers. It reaffirms the transformative power of faith in adversity, showing that trials are opportunities for God's love to shine even brighter. The depth of God's love becomes more evident, and the strength He provides is more palpable when we see others thrive through their hardships.

Walking in victory and freedom: To walk in victory and freedom means embodying the triumph of faith over fear. David, who battled addiction for years, finally found freedom through his faith in Christ. Upon embracing his identity as a conqueror in Christ, he often reflected on Philippians 4:13, "I can do all this through him who gives me strength." This verse became his anthem, empowering him to face each day with renewed courage.

Here's how you can embrace this victorious mindset:

- Regularly affirm your identity in Christ through positive declarations.
- Memorize and meditate on scriptures that reinforce your victory over challenges.
- Share your victories with others to create a ripple effect of

encouragement and faith.

Through faith, readers can confidently navigate life's storms, knowing that God's grace is more than sufficient for every trial. Embracing this mindset allows you to transcend earthly challenges, walking boldly in the freedom Christ offers.

By immersing ourselves in the testimonies of those who've weathered life's storms and extracting valuable lessons from their journeys, we become equipped to face our challenges with resilience, trust, and unwavering faith. The transformative power of God's grace molds us into vessels of His unending love and mercy, ready to walk in victory and freedom no matter the storms. (University, C., 2024) (How To Embrace and Overcome Adversity. proverbs31.org., n.d.)

Cultivating faith, resilience, and victory through Christ

This chapter explored how life's challenges and storms are not just random occurrences but purposeful elements in our journey. By looking at examples from the Bible like Job, Joseph, and Paul, we've seen how enduring trials can lead to spiritual growth and deeper faith. These stories teach us that maintaining faith and trusting in God's plan can bring about amazing transformation, even in the darkest times.

Understanding that God uses these tough times to refine our character helps us face them with more courage and resilience. Seeing our struggles as opportunities for growth changes our perspective and strengthens our trust in God. This chapter has also given practical advice on navigating these storms, such as prayer, scripture study, serving others, and keeping a journal of our experiences.

It's important to remember that challenges help us grow spiritually and mature in our faith. They act as a refining fire, much like gold being purified by intense heat. This process, although painful, is necessary to reveal our true potential and deepen our relationship with God. Perseverance through these trials leads to a stronger, more resilient faith.

We develop a new appreciation for the journey as we embrace the lessons learned during difficult times. Each trial brings the opportunity for profound personal and spiritual insights, drawing us closer to God. It's not just about surviving the storm but thriving and emerging as a stronger individual.

Ultimately, life's storms are meant to transform us. They push us to rely more on God's providence and less on our understanding. By facing these challenges with faith, we open ourselves up to incredible growth and renewed purpose. So, the next time you find yourself in the midst of a storm, remember that it's part of a bigger picture designed for your growth. Embrace the journey, trust in God's plan, and recognize each challenge as an opportunity to become the person God intends you to be.

Chapter Two.

Breaking Free From Fear and Doubt

Imagine going through life's toughest moments without any form of guidance or support. It can feel like navigating a stormy sea in a small boat tossed around by the waves with no safe harbor in sight. But what if you had an anchor to keep you steady? That anchor is a strong faith foundation that offers stability and hope when everything else feels uncertain.

Living without a robust faith foundation can be challenging. Many people struggle with feelings of anxiety and fear, especially when faced with unexpected difficulties. These emotions can become overwhelming, leading to a sense of helplessness. For example, someone who loses their job might feel panicked about the future, questioning their worth and purpose. Without a solid faith foundation, finding peace and assurance during such tumultuous times becomes hard. Daily stresses and larger life challenges alike can easily derail a person, leaving them feeling lost and ungrounded.

In this chapter, we will explore practical steps to strengthen your faith foundation so you can better withstand life's storms. We'll delve into daily devotional practices and how they can ground you in your faith. You'll learn about the power of scriptural meditation and its role in providing comfort and strength. Finally, we will discuss the importance of fostering a consistent prayer life. By the end of this chapter, you'll have the tools and insights needed to build a resilient faith foundation, helping you navigate whatever life throws your way with confidence and peace.

Importance of Daily Devotional Practices

Building a robust faith foundation to withstand life's storms is a journey that requires consistent effort and dedication. One of the most impactful practices in this journey is maintaining daily devotions. Daily devotional practices are not just rituals; they are powerful tools that ground our faith and provide perspective amid life's inevitable challenges.

Consistent devotional practices help foster spiritual growth by encouraging us to seek God's daily presence. This regular engagement with God nurtures an intimate connection that strengthens our faith. Establishing such a habit is essential, as it cultivates a deep sense of trust and reliance on God's guidance. To develop a habit of devotion:

- Start by setting aside a specific time each day dedicated to your devotion.

- Choose a quiet spot where you can focus without distractions.

- Select a holy book or scripture passage to guide your daily sessions.

Another cornerstone of building a strong faith foundation is scriptural meditation. Regularly meditating on key scriptures reinforces our faith and provides strength during times of need. Reflecting deeply on these passages helps deepen our understanding of God's promises and faithfulness. It brings about clarity and peace, especially during difficult seasons. Here's how to incorporate scriptural meditation into your routine:

- Begin by selecting specific verses that resonate with you.

- Spend a few minutes reading and rereading the passage, allowing the words to sink in.

- Reflect on what these verses mean in the context of your current life situation.

- Pray and ask for insight and understanding, letting the scriptures speak to you personally.

Scriptural meditation not only clarifies but also empowers believers to face adversity with confidence.

By internalizing key passages, we prepare ourselves mentally and spiritually to handle any tough situations that come our way. Consistently engaging with scriptures and reflecting on their meanings helps anchor us in our faith, making it more resilient against the storms of life.

Consistency in these daily devotions and scriptural meditations fosters a robust faith foundation. It's about creating a reliable routine that becomes second nature, turning to God daily for guidance and strength. Over time, these practices build a fortress of faith that stands firm regardless of our external challenges.

In summary, readers will grasp the significance of daily devotions and scriptural meditation in fortifying their faith foundation. These practices are not mere religious obligations but essential tools for grounding one's faith and providing perspective amidst life's trials. By establishing a habit of devotion and regularly meditating on scriptures, we nurture an intimate connection with God that empowers us to face life's adversities with unwavering confidence.

(Willis, A., 2016)

Impact of Key Scriptures

Key scriptures play a critical role when building a robust faith foundation to withstand life's storms. Verses such as

Philippians 4:13 and Isaiah 41:10 offer reassurance and strength during challenging times. They serve as beacons of hope, anchoring believers in

God's promises and plans. Memorizing and internalizing these scriptures equips us to stand firm in our beliefs when trials come our way.

Here is what you can do to achieve this:

- Find verses that resonate with you personally and speak to your heart and current life circumstances.

- Write them down or keep them handy on your phone for easy access.

- Recite them regularly, especially during moments of doubt or fear, letting the words sink deep into your soul.

Applying biblical truths transforms superficial faith into unwavering conviction. When we actively implement scriptures in our daily lives, it builds a resilient foundation. It means living out principles like love, mercy, forgiveness, and trust in God's provision. This not only strengthens our personal faith but also serves as a testament to others.

To do this effectively:

- Start your day by reading and reflecting on a Bible passage that speaks to your current situation or mindset.

- Look for practical ways to apply what you've read throughout the day.

- Keep a journal of how these applications impact your life and your faith journey.

Living out biblical truths reinforces trust in God's promises and provisions. It requires consistent effort and mindfulness to put these teachings into action. Practicing patience, kindness, and humility even when it's hard shows true reliance on God's guidance.

Here are steps to guide you:

- During difficult moments, pause and ask yourself how biblical principles can be applied to the situation.

- Actively choose responses and actions that align with these principles, even if they go against your initial reaction.

- Reflect on how these choices affect your sense of peace and trust in God's plan.

Implementing scriptures actively in daily life fosters a resilient faith foundation. Living by these doctrines ensures that faith is more than just words—it becomes a lifestyle rooted in divine wisdom and truth. This practice not only fortifies individual faith but also inspires others.

Steps to encourage this include:

- Engage in regular study groups or discussions where you can learn from others and share your insights.

- Make time for daily devotionals that delve deeply into Scripture.

- Set reminders to keep your thoughts aligned with biblical teachings throughout the day.

A strong faith foundation doesn't happen overnight. It's built through continual learning, reflection, and application of God's word. Taking these principles to heart ensures that when life's storms hit, you'll be grounded and unshaken, confident in the strength of a deep-rooted faith.

Role of Community Support

Being part of a faith community is a true blessing, especially when it comes to building a robust faith foundation to withstand life's storms. Let's dive into how community support within the church can significantly nurture and strengthen your faith.

One of the most impactful aspects of being in a faith community is the encouragement you receive from supportive relationships. When you share your struggles and victories with fellow believers, you foster a sense of unity and encouragement. This isn't just about talking; it's about genuinely connecting and relating to each other's experiences. Sharing your journey openly creates bonds that uplift and motivate everyone involved.

Here is what you can do to achieve this:

- Be open and honest about your experiences.

- Listen actively and provide empathy to others.

- Celebrate victories together, no matter how small they may seem.

- Offer and accept help during tough times.

Engaging with a faith community provides immense emotional and spiritual support during challenging times. When you're part of a group that truly cares, you're never alone in your trials. The community's collective strength helps lighten burdens and offers a safe space to express fears and doubts. The support system within the church can lead to healing and provide the resilience needed to face life's adversities.

The church shares diverse perspectives and insights, which can deepen your faith journey. Hearing different viewpoints and interpretations of Scripture enriches your understanding and can offer fresh revelations about your own faith. It encourages growth by challenging you to look at things from varying angles and deepening your connection with God. This diversity fosters a broader comprehension of faith and promotes personal development.

Now, let's talk about accountability and growth, which are also crucial components of community support. Accountability partners can help individuals stay focused on their faith goals and commitments. These partners remind you of your aspirations, encourage consistency, and provide gentle nudges when you veer off track. It's about mutual support, where both parties benefit from staying committed to their faith practices.

To make the most out of your accountability partnerships:

- Choose someone you trust and who shares similar faith values.

- Set clear, achievable goals together.

- Regularly check in with each other.

- Be open to feedback and willing to provide constructive input.

Engaging with other believers in the church leads to mutual improvement and shared spiritual growth. Participating in group studies, worship sessions, and prayer meetings allows for collective learning and spiritual elevation. Each member's growth contributes to the overall strengthening of the community, creating an environment where everyone thrives spiritually.

Community support is a pillar of strength in navigating life's storms with faith and resilience. Knowing there's a network of believers backing you up instills confidence and assurance. The combined wisdom and experience within the community offer practical advice and spiritual guidance, helping you maintain steadfast faith even in turbulent times. This kind of support transforms churches into sanctuaries of hope and places of refuge.

In summary, seeking and providing community support within the church is foundational in strengthening your faith for enduring life's challenges. Embracing these supportive relationships, engaging with diverse perspectives, holding each other accountable, and collectively growing spiritually will undoubtedly build a robust faith foundation. This community involvement fortifies individual belief systems and creates a cohesive, resilient body of believers ready to face any storm together.

Significance of Consistent Prayer Life

Building a robust faith foundation requires more than just passive belief; it demands active practices that keep faith alive and strong. One of the most significant ways to fortify one's faith is through developing a consistent prayer life.

Prayer as a Foundation

Prayer acts as the cornerstone in building and reinforcing faith, especially amid life's trials. Engaging in regular communication with God through prayer strengthens the bond of trust and creates a sense of dependence on Him. When you consistently pray, you foster a sense of peace and assurance in God's presence and guidance. This is crucial during challenging times when the world feels chaotic and unstable. Dependence on prayer cultivates a posture of surrender, aligning oneself with God's plan and will.

Types of Prayer Practices

Introducing various prayer methods can greatly aid spiritual growth and resilience. Here's what you can do to incorporate different types of prayers into your routine:

- **Intercessory Prayers**: Pray for yourself and others. This fosters empathy and compassion, particularly during difficult times.

- **Petition Prayers**: Articulate your personal needs and desires to God. This practice encourages vulnerability and deepens your trust in Him.

- **Thanksgiving Prayers**: Cultivate a heart of gratitude by acknowledging God's faithfulness even amidst trials. This helps maintain a positive outlook and reinforces the belief that God is always at work.

By engaging in these different types of prayers, you create a well-rounded prayer life that supports spiritual growth and helps you stand firm during life's storms.

Key Takeaways

We've journeyed through the importance of daily devotional practices and how they can build a strong faith foundation to help us weather life's storms. These practices aren't just rituals but powerful tools that ground our faith, providing much-needed perspective during difficult times. We've explored the significance of setting aside time each day for devotion, finding quiet spots free from distractions, and choosing meaningful scripture passages to guide our sessions.

Reflecting on key scriptures and meditating on their meanings is another cornerstone in fortifying our belief system. This regular engagement with God's word deepens our understanding of His promises, bringing clarity and peace, especially during tough seasons. By internalizing these passages, we prepare ourselves to face adversity with confidence. It's all about fostering a consistent, daily routine that becomes second nature, helping us turn to God for guidance and strength.

In addition to personal devotions, living out biblical truths is crucial. Finding verses that resonate with your heart and applying them in everyday actions transforms superficial faith into unwavering conviction. Implementing these teachings in real-life situations ensures that faith is more than just words— it's a lifestyle rooted in divine wisdom and truth.

Being part of a faith community adds another layer of support. Sharing struggles and victories with fellow believers fosters unity and encouragement. This communal bond provides emotional and spiritual support and diverse perspectives that enrich your faith journey. Accountability partners and group studies contribute to mutual edification and shared growth, making the community a true pillar of strength.

Consistent prayer life ties everything together, acting as a cornerstone in building and reinforcing faith. Engaging in various types of prayers—whether intercessory, petition, or thanksgiving—creates a well-rounded communication with God. This practice strengthens trust, surrender, and gratitude, which are essential when facing life's storms.

Building a robust faith foundation is a multifaceted journey requiring daily devotion, scriptural meditation, actionable faith, community support, and consistent prayer. It's a continual process of learning, reflecting, and applying God's word. Strengthening this foundation ensures that when life's challenges arise, we remain grounded and unshaken, confident in the steadfastness of our faith. As you continue on this path, remember that every small step taken today helps build a fortress of faith ready to withstand tomorrow's storms.

Chapter Three.

Embracing God's Peace

Fear and doubt can feel like chains holding you back from living fully. Imagine wanting to take a leap of faith, but you're stuck, gripped by what-ifs and negative thoughts. We all go through moments where fear and doubt creep in and start to control our decisions. Breaking free isn't easy, but it's entirely possible.

Consider how past experiences shape your present fears. Maybe a harsh word from someone you trusted made you question your worth, or a failed project made you doubt your abilities. These lingering fears don't just vanish; they influence how you see yourself and the world around you. On top of that, societal pressures add another layer, making you compare yourself with others' successes. It's tough to keep your own path when it feels like everyone else is racing ahead. Recognizing these sources of fear and learning to confront them is a big step toward breaking their hold on you.

In this chapter, we'll identify the roots of your fears and doubts and explore practical ways to overcome them. You'll see how understanding past influences and external pressures can help you reclaim your confidence. We will also offer guidance on

41

differentiating between healthy caution and paralyzing fear so you can navigate challenges with a clear mind. By the end, you'll have strategies to tackle these feelings head-on, embracing God's promises with newfound assurance and freedom.

Identifying sources of fear and doubt

Understanding how past experiences and negative influences contribute to fear and doubt is an important first step. We all have moments in our lives that leave lasting marks—whether it's a harsh word from someone we trusted or a failure we couldn't control. These past events can create lingering fears that shape our current beliefs and actions. For instance, if you've experienced rejection, you might now doubt your worth and potential. Breaking free means acknowledging these experiences and seeing them for what they are: pieces of the past that don't define your future.

Societal pressures and external factors also play a significant role in fueling fear and doubt. We live in a world full of expectations—from career milestones to social media highlights—that create undue pressure. Constant comparisons to others' successes or societal standards can make us doubt our own paths. Understanding that much of this pressure is external and learning to focus on your personal journey is crucial. Try to remember that your value doesn't come from conforming to outside expectations but from being true to yourself and your faith.

It's essential to differentiate between healthy caution and paralyzing fear. Healthy caution helps us stay safe and prepared; that little voice reminds us to look both ways before crossing the street. Paralyzing fear, on the other hand, stops us from living fully and embracing God's promises. It can make small challenges seem insurmountable and prevent us from taking necessary steps forward.

Here is what you can do to discern between healthy caution and paralyzing fear:

- First, reflect on the root of your concern. Is it based on tangible risks or just "what if" scenarios?

- Second, seek counsel from trusted friends or mentors who can offer perspective and wisdom.

- Third, practice grounding techniques such as deep breathing or prayer to calm your mind.

- Fourth, take gradual steps towards facing your fears to build confidence over time.

By understanding where your fears and doubts originate, recognizing the external pressures adding to them, and learning to identify what's holding you back, you'll be better equipped to combat them with faith. Remember, overcoming these feelings isn't about ignoring them but addressing them head-on with the confidence that comes from faith in God's promises. By tackling these areas, you're paving the way to live more freely and authentically, fully embracing the life God has planned for you.

Biblical promises that counteract fear

Overcoming fear and doubt to embrace God's promises with confidence Fear can be a crippling emotion that holds us back from experiencing the fullness of God's promises. And yet, throughout the Bible, we find verses overflowing with assurances of God's faithfulness and protection in times of trouble. It's like having an anchor during a storm; these promises are meant to stabilize and reassure us.

Think about Isaiah 41:10, which says, "Do not fear, for I am with you; do not be dismayed, for I am your God. I will strengthen you and help you; I will uphold you with my righteous right hand." This verse is a direct call from God, reminding us that we don't have to face our troubles alone. This divine assurance allows us to lean on His strength rather than our own.

Another powerful scripture is in Psalm 23:4, "Even though I walk through the valley of the shadow of death, I will fear no evil, for you are with me; your rod and your staff, they comfort me." Here, we're reminded that God is with us through the darkest times. The imagery of God's rod and staff provides a tangible sense of security, depicting God's guidance and protection.

Trust and reliance on God's sovereignty form another bedrock in combating fear and doubt. Proverbs 3:5-6 encourages us to "Trust in the Lord with all your heart and lean not on your own understanding; in all your ways submit to him, and he will make your paths straight." Trusting God means acknowledging His control over our lives and believing His plans for us are good, even when we can't see the full picture.

Jeremiah 29:11 further emphasizes this, "For I know the plans I have for you," declares the Lord, "plans to prosper you and not to harm you, plans to give you hope and a future." This verse helps us shift our focus from immediate concerns to God's broader vision for our lives, fostering a sense of peace and purpose.

Freedom from fear through faith is also a recurring theme in the New Testament. In 2 Timothy 1:7, Paul writes, "For God has not given us a spirit of fear, but of power and of love and of a sound mind." This Scripture motivates us to recognize that fear is not from God and has no place in our hearts. By focusing on the power, love, and sound mind that God gives us, we can confront and conquer our fears.

Additionally, 1 John 4:18 says, "There is no fear in love. But perfect love drives out fear because fear has to do with punishment. The one who fears is not made perfect in love." This verse underscores the transformative power of God's love, which can eradicate fear entirely. It invites us to dwell in the perfection of God's love, which brings freedom and tranquility.

By meditating on these passages, we align ourselves with God's truth, enabling us to stand firm against fear and doubt. When Scripture declares that faith can move mountains, it's not just a metaphor. Our faith in God's promises equips us with an unshakeable foundation, providing the confidence needed to face life's challenges.

The key takeaways for readers are clear: immerse yourself in biblical truths as a defense against fear. Equip yourself with these promises, letting them be the lens through which you view your trials and uncertainties. By doing so, you anchor your faith in a God who is faithful, protective, and whose love casts out all fear. This divine assurance transforms our outlook, turning potential moments of fear into opportunities for faith to flourish.

As you engage with these scriptures, remember that overcoming fear and doubt isn't a one-time event but a continuous journey of faith. Keep returning to God's Word, let it fill your heart and mind, and watch how it empowers you to live boldly and confidently in His promises.

Practical steps to renew your mind

Overcoming fear and doubt to embrace God's promises confidently is a journey that requires practical steps to renew your mind and shift your focus from fear to faith. Here are some actionable strategies to help you cultivate a mindset of faith and confidence:

Implementing daily affirmations of faith and trust in God: Start each day by affirming your faith and trust in God's promises. This practice can transform your mindset over time by reinforcing positive, faith-based beliefs.

- Begin by choosing a few affirmations grounded in Scripture, such as "I can do all things through Christ who strengthens me" (Philippians 4:13) or "God has not given us a spirit of fear, but of power and love and a sound mind" (2 Timothy 1:7).

- Write these affirmations on sticky notes and place them where you'll see them often, like your bathroom mirror, car dashboard, or computer monitor.

- Repeat these affirmations out loud every morning and throughout the day to remind yourself of God's promises.

Engaging in mindfulness practices to redirect negative thought patterns Mindfulness is a powerful tool to help you become aware of your thoughts and redirect them toward faith and positivity.

- Practice deep breathing exercises to calm your mind and center your thoughts on God's peace.

- Spend a few minutes each day in quiet meditation, focusing on a specific scripture or listening for God's guidance.

- When negative thoughts arise, acknowledge them without judgment and gently guide your focus back to a positive, faith-filled perspective. For instance, if you worry about the future, remind yourself of Jeremiah 29:11 – "For I know the plans I have for you, declares the Lord, plans to prosper you and not to harm you, plans to give you hope and a future."

Seeking accountability and support to stay aligned with faith-based perspectives Having a support system can make a significant difference in maintaining your focus on faith rather than fear.

- Join a small group or Bible study where you can share your struggles and victories with others who are also striving to grow in their faith.

- Find a trusted friend or mentor to whom you can turn for encouragement and prayer when doubts creep in.

- Make a habit of praying for and with your accountability partner, lifting each other up and reminding one another of God's promises.

By implementing these practical steps, you can renew your mind and shift your focus from fear to faith. Engaging in daily affirmations, mindfulness practices, and seeking accountability are key actions that will help you cultivate a mindset rooted in faith and confidence. Over time, these habits will empower you to overcome fear and doubt, allowing you to embrace God's promises with boldness and assurance.

In summary, renewing your mind is not an overnight process but a continuous journey. By surrounding yourself with God's truth and staying connected with a community that uplifts your faith, you create an environment where fear and doubt cannot thrive. Remember, it's about progress, not perfection. No matter how small, each step you take leads you closer to living a life filled with faith and confidence in God's promises.

Testimonies of overcoming fear through faith

Overcoming fear and doubt to embrace God's promises confidently can be a transformative journey. Let's dive into some real-life stories highlighting how unwavering faith can conquer paralyzing fear, encouraging you to trust in God's power.

Let's start with Heather's story. Heather, a long-time believer, faced a life-altering surgery at thirteen. A mysterious cyst was found pressing on her brain, a discovery that led to an emergency operation. While the procedure was a success, Heather's brush with mortality left her in perpetual fear. She constantly worried about losing her job, not having enough money, or having a car accident. It wasn't until she recalled the words from 2 Timothy 1:7, "God has not given us a spirit of fear, but of power and of love and of a sound mind," that she decided to combat her fears actively. She prayed fervently each time fear took hold, asking God for strength and a sound mind. Gradually, she saw tremendous victory over fear, learning to place her life entirely in God's hands and trust His plans for her future ("Here's how I found freedom from fear. Active Christianity., 2020).

Similarly, let's talk about Scott. He shares his experience of overcoming the fear of making wrong decisions. At one point, he was dating a girl but stopped pursuing the relationship out of fear. This fear led him to miss out on what could have been a wonderful partnership. Reflecting on this missed opportunity, Scott realized the need to remove fear through faith. Later, while dating someone else, they were stuck together in a car during a snowstorm. The extended conversation helped dissolve his fears, and he understood that facing future uncertainty with faith allowed him to see God's hand guiding him.

Another compelling narrative involves a father sharing how past mistakes haunted his daughter. She worried that being sent to the principal's office in first grade would adversely affect her entire future. Her fears stemmed from believing she wasn't perfect. Through numerous discussions, he helped her understand the importance of repentance and belief in the Atonement of Jesus Christ. They read Boyd K. Packer's assurance that true repentance leaves no scars, emphasizing that God forgives once we repent sincerely. This teaching brought her immense relief and hope for a bright future, unshackled from past mistakes.

These stories serve as powerful examples of how faith in God's promises leads to victorious outcomes. When Heather prayed and asked for help, God replaced her fears with love and hope. Scott's story teaches us that acting in faith, even when scared, makes God's guidance evident. The father's lesson illustrates how understanding and embracing the Atonement can free us from the burden of past errors.

Stepping out in faith, despite initial trepidation, is another crucial aspect. Imagine being called to relocate by divine instruction like the early members of the Church in New York, who were commanded to move to Ohio. Faced with uncertainty, they feared uprooting their lives. Yet, the Lord promised them that His eyes were upon them and that they would eventually see Him in their lives. Acting on faith, despite their fears, opened doors to unimaginable blessings.

Overcoming fear through faith isn't just about monumental life changes. It's also about everyday decisions and trusting God in smaller matters. One must remember that faith grows through constant practice. As we encounter daily uncertainties, turning to prayer and scriptures for comfort and guidance helps reinforce our trust in God.

So, what can you take away from these experiences? First, recognize that fear is natural but not impossible. By leaning on prayer, Scripture, and community, you can develop a strong faith to tackle any fear. Second, understand that past mistakes do not define your future. Embrace God's forgiveness and move forward confidently. Lastly, don't be afraid to take small steps of faith in your daily life. These small acts build a foundation of trust in God, preparing you for bigger leaps of faith.

In conclusion, real-life testimonies show us that unwavering faith is the key to overcoming fear. Whether it's Heather confronting her lifelong anxieties, Scott navigating relationship fears, or a father helping his daughter overcome guilt, faith in God's promises brings victory. Let these stories inspire you to face your fears with boldness, knowing that with faith, you can confidently embrace God's promises.

What does this mean?

We've talked about how fear and doubt can creep into our lives, shaped by past experiences and the pressures of society. We've also examined how grounding ourselves in God's promises helps us overcome these feelings. Remember how we discussed that just because something happened in the past doesn't mean it defines our future? That's a key point to take away.

Right now, we're standing at a crossroads. We've identified where our fears come from and how they hold us back. It's time to choose faith over fear. Imagine your life without the weight of these doubts. What would you do differently? How much freer would you feel?

For some readers, this might seem easier said than done. Breaking free from fear isn't an overnight process. It's understandable if you're concerned about slipping back into old patterns. The journey to overcoming fear and doubt is ongoing, and there will be challenges along the way.

On a larger scale, imagine what could happen if more people confidently embraced God's promises.

Societies could change, communities could become stronger, and personal relationships could thrive. When individuals are no longer held back by fear, they can step into their true potential and positively impact the world around them.

So, what's next for you? Take a moment to think about the steps you've learned to face your fears and doubts. Each small step forward counts. Embrace the support of your community, lean into God's promises, and remember that this journey is ongoing. The more you practice, the more natural it becomes to live confidently in God's love and assurance. Keep moving forward with faith, and watch how the landscape of your life begins to change.

Chapter Four.

The Power of Prayer in

Adversity

Finding peace can feel like chasing a butterfly sometimes. You know it's there, but it's elusive, slipping away just when you think you've caught it. Amid the hustle and chaos of everyday life, many of us long for a sense of tranquility. Yet, we often look for peace in our surroundings or circumstances, hoping that a change in situation will calm our hearts and minds.

The problem is that the worldly peace is fragile and temporary. Picture trying to relax after a long day only to be interrupted by urgent work emails or family demands. Or consider how easily your peace can shatter with unexpected bad news or financial stress. In contrast, God's peace offers something deeper and unshakeable, regardless of external turmoil. Consider biblical figures like Daniel, who remained composed in a den of lions, or Paul and Silas, who sang hymns while imprisoned. Their secret wasn't an absence of trouble but a profound inner peace rooted in their trust in God.

This chapter dives into the journey of finding and maintaining God's peace during turbulent times. We'll explore how to recognize this divine peace and understand its nature. We'll discuss practical steps like practicing gratitude, trusting God, and surrendering control. You'll also learn how prayer, meditation, and reflection are crucial in nurturing a peaceful heart. By the end, you'll have a roadmap to experience and hold on to God's peace, even when life feels overwhelming.

Understanding the Peace of God

Understanding the peace of God means noticing its presence even when chaos reigns. God's peace is like an anchor, steady and constant, even when everything around you feels tumultuous. It's a tranquility that goes beyond what we can logically grasp, offering a supernatural calm that keeps us grounded.

Worldly peace often depends on circumstances, but God's peace remains steadfast regardless of the situation. Consider biblical figures like Daniel in the lion's den or Paul and Silas singing hymns in prison. These individuals found unwavering peace amid their trials because they trusted in God's promises.

The next step is connecting contentment and trust with experiencing God's peace. Practicing gratitude can shift our mindset significantly. Being grateful, even for small things, brings about a sense of contentment. Here's how to nurture this:

- Start by listing things you're thankful for each day.

- Focus on the positives, no matter how minor they seem.

- Remind yourself regularly of the blessings you've received.

Trusting God is another critical aspect. His promises include provision, protection, and peace. To foster this trust:

- Reflect on times when God has come through for you.

- Pray specifically for greater faith in His promises.

- Surround yourself with stories of God's faithfulness, whether through Scripture or testimonies from others.

A huge part of finding peace involves surrendering control. Clinging too tightly to our plans can create anxiety. Instead, try these steps for letting go:

- Identify areas where you're holding on too tightly.

- Pray, asking God to help you release control.

- Practice saying, "God, I trust You with this," whenever you feel the urge to regain control.

Engaging in prayer and meditation are excellent ways to maintain this inner peace. Prayer allows us to hand over our worries to God. For peace of mind:

- Set aside specific times each day to pray.

- Speak candidly to God about your concerns.

- Trust that He hears you and is working things out.

Meditation helps to center our thoughts on God's peace. Here's a guide to incorporating it into your routine:

- Find a quiet place where you won't be disturbed.

- Focus on a scripture or a phrase that brings peace.

- Take deep breaths and let go of distracting thoughts.

Silence and reflection also play crucial roles. You create space to hear from God by carving out time for silence. Consider these practices:

- Dedicate a few minutes each morning to sit quietly.

- Reflect on what God might be telling you through your day.

- Use a journal to note down insights and peaceful moments.

You can find a deeper sense of serenity by understanding God's peace, trusting in His promises, surrendering control, and engaging in prayer and meditation. Remember, God's peace is accessible even when life feels overwhelming. It's about turning your focus toward Him and allowing His presence to transform your outlook.

Scriptural Assurance of God's Peace

Philippians 4:6-7 – Pray without ceasing: Understanding the power of prayer in experiencing God's peace that surpasses understanding.

Prayer has an extraordinary power to bring us into God's peace, even when everything around us seems chaotic. This Scripture encourages us to bring all our worries and supplications to God. When we pray, it's not just about asking for things but also creating a connection with God and letting go of what burdens us.

- Pour out your concerns and leave them in God's hands.

- Trust that He is listening and working on your behalf.

- Embrace peace by knowing you're never alone in your struggles.

Trusting in God's faithfulness and His promise to guard hearts and minds with peace is essential. When we're overwhelmed, taking our anxieties to God can provide relief and comfort that surpasses any human understanding.

John 14:27 – Peace I leave with you: Exploring Jesus' assurance of peace as a gift to His followers.

Jesus said, "Peace I leave with you; my peace I give you." This peace isn't contingent on our circumstances but is a gift originating from Christ Himself. During trials, internalizing these words can be immensely comforting.

- Reflect on how Christ's peace is different from worldly peace.

- Imagine this divine peace filling your heart and mind.

- Allow this peace to replace fear and anxiety, recognizing it as a precious gift from Jesus.

Isaiah 26:3 – You keep them in perfect peace: Delving into the concept of perfect peace found in unwavering trust in God.

Perfect peace comes from unwavering trust in God. Isaiah 26:3 promises that those who focus their minds steadfastly on God will remain in perfect peace. Trusting God means letting go of our need for control and believing in His divine plans.

- Focus daily on God's goodness and faithfulness.

- Practice shifting your thoughts to God's promises whenever worry creeps in.

- Internalize this promise by meditating on it regularly, grounding yourself in His unwavering peace.

Psalm 29:11 – The Lord gives strength to his people: Connecting God's peace with His provision of strength and stability in times of trouble.

The Lord promises strength and peace to His people,

offering us stability in troubled times. Drawing on this empowerment helps us navigate life's storms without losing our sense of peace.

- Remember God's past provisions and let them assure you.

- Lean on His strength rather than your own during difficult times.

- Use His peace as a foundation to face challenges with courage.

By anchoring ourselves in these scriptures, we can find tangible, accessible peace no matter the chaos surrounding us. This peace doesn't come from the absence of problems but from the presence of God in our lives.

Worship, Praise, and Gratitude

Finding and maintaining God's peace during turbulent times can feel challenging, but worship, praise, and gratitude provide pathways to that peace. Let's look at how these practices create an atmosphere where God's peace can thrive.

Worship as a pathway to peace means seeing it as a transformative practice that ushers in God's presence and calm. Worship isn't just about singing or praying; it's a way to express our adoration and reverence for

God acknowledging His sovereignty and trustworthiness,

especially amid trials. When we actively engage in worship, we open ourselves up to experience God's peaceful presence. Here's what you can do:

- Make time daily for personal worship through singing, prayer, or quiet reflection.

- Focus on God's attributes like His goodness, mercy, and power.

- Let worship be a reminder that God is greater than any challenge you face.

The power of gratitude and praise is profound. Gratitude changes our perspective, helping us shift our focus from challenges to blessings. Research shows that practicing gratitude activates brain regions associated with positive emotions and even strengthens our immune system (The Power Of Gratitude | Full Strength Network, n.d.). This makes gratitude a powerful tool in combating anxiety and fear. Here's a practical approach:

- Keep a gratitude journal. Each day, write down three things you're thankful for.

- Verbally praise and thank God throughout your day, even for small blessings.

- Use praise as spiritual warfare; when anxiety and fear arise, counter them with thanksgiving.

Maintaining a posture of praise involves making praise a lifestyle, not just an occasional activity. This consistent practice invites God's peace into all areas of life. Here are some steps to incorporate regular praise:

- Set aside specific times each day for praise sessions, like during your commute or before bed.

- Create playlists of worship music to listen to while doing daily tasks.

- Encourage family members to join in regular times of corporate praise and worship.

Recognizing the role of praise helps shift the atmosphere around us, creating spaces where God's peace can dwell even in challenging situations. Here's how:

- Start meetings or gatherings with a moment of praise and thanksgiving.

- In difficult moments, pause to praise God aloud for His past faithfulness and future promises.

- Surround yourself with reminders of God's promises and testimonies of His goodness.

Taking these steps to integrate worship, praise, and gratitude into your daily routine can create a continuous source of peace. By focusing on these practices, you'll find that God's peace becomes more accessible, anchoring you through life's storms.

Mindfulness and Gratitude Practices

Finding and maintaining God's peace during turbulent times is a journey that involves the critical practices of mindfulness and gratitude. These practices can serve as anchors, helping us remain grounded in God's peace despite life's chaos.

Mindfulness Practices for Peace

Mindfulness techniques can be powerful tools to help us stay grounded in the present moment and experience God's peace. Mindfulness allows us to combat anxiety and uncertainty by focusing on the here and now.

Practicing awareness and presence: When we practice being aware and present, it helps redirect our thoughts from chaos to God's sovereignty. For example:

- Take time each day to pause and notice your environment. Observe the sounds, sights, and sensations around you.

- Use breathing exercises to center your mind. As you breathe in, say a phrase like "God's peace," as you breathe out, say "is with me."

Utilizing mindfulness exercises: Engaging in these exercises can help us shift our focus away from worries and towards the reassurance of God's control and presence.

Gratitude as a Game-Changer

Cultivating a heart of gratitude profoundly impacts our peace and perspective. Gratitude transforms our mindset, allowing us to recognize and cherish God's blessings despite challenges.

Keeping a gratitude journal: Recording moments of grace helps foster a habit of thankfulness.

- Every evening, write down three things you are grateful for. They don't have to be grand; sometimes, small blessings hold the most power.

- Reflect on how these blessings remind you of God's love and provision.

Recognizing the link between gratitude and contentment: A thankful heart leads to contentment, which fosters an inner sense of peace.

- Whenever you feel stressed, take a moment to think about the positives in your life and thank God for them. This shifts your focus from what's lacking to what's abundant.

Creating a Peaceful Environment

Implementing practical steps to create a physical and mental space conducive to experiencing God's peace is essential. Here are some ways to achieve this:

Establishing daily rhythms and practices:

- Begin your day with prayer and meditation, focusing on God's promises.

- Set aside specific times for quiet reflection and mindfulness exercises.

- *Surrounding yourself with reminders of God's faithfulness:*

- Decorate your living and working spaces with verses or images that remind you of God's promises.

- Keep symbols of faith, such as crosses or inspirational artwork, where you can see them daily.

By engaging in mindfulness exercises, embracing gratitude, and creating environments that foster peace, we can enhance our experience of God's peace even amidst life's storms. Remember, these practices are not just routines but pathways to deeper faith and tranquility.

Key Takeaways

Throughout this chapter, we've explored finding and maintaining God's peace during turbulent times. We started by understanding how God's peace is an anchor, steady, and constant even when everything around us is chaotic. Examples like Daniel in the lion's den and Paul and Silas singing hymns in prison highlighted how such peace is attainable regardless of our circumstances.

We then looked at practical ways to connect contentment and trust with experiencing God's peace. Practicing gratitude and trusting in God's promises are key factors. We can foster a sense of peace and contentment by listing things we're thankful for each day and reflecting on times when God has shown His faithfulness. Surrendering control and engaging in regular prayer and meditation are vital in maintaining this inner tranquility.

Turning to Scripture shows us that God's peace surpasses all understanding, as seen in Philippians, John, Isaiah, and Psalms passages. These scriptures provide assurance and a reminder that God's peace is a gift available to all believers, no matter their situations.

Worship, praise, and gratitude further reinforce our connection to God's peace. Regularly engaging in worship and maintaining a posture of praise creates an atmosphere where God's presence feels nearer and more comforting. Gratitude helps shift our focus from challenges to blessings, making seeing and feeling God's peace easier.

Finally, incorporating mindfulness and gratitude practices into our daily lives helps maintain that sense of serenity. Simple techniques like mindfulness exercises and keeping a gratitude journal make it easier to stay grounded and aware of God's blessings, even amid life's chaos.

Remember, achieving and maintaining God's peace is a journey, not a one-time event. While life's storms are inevitable, the peace of God remains a steadfast anchor. So, let's take these tools and practices to heart, knowing they'll help us navigate through any turbulent times ahead.

Chapter Five.

Walking in Spiritual Authority

Ever felt like you're navigating a storm with no end in sight? That's when we often find ourselves seeking anything to hold onto. Prayer can be that anchor, offering peace and strength when everything feels chaotic. It's not just about asking for help. It's about connecting with something greater than ourselves and tapping into a source of hope and resilience.

When adversity strikes, it can be paralyzing. Whether it's the loss of a job, a health crisis, or relational strife, these moments test our limits. Imagine losing your job, feeling the weight of financial instability, and not knowing how to make ends meet. Or consider facing a serious illness where each day brings uncertainty and fear. These are the times when faith can waver, and we struggle to see a way forward. It's easy to feel isolated and overwhelmed, questioning if there's any relief in sight.

In these challenging seasons, prayer can be transformative.

This chapter explores various prayers that can help us navigate adversity. We'll delve into prayers of supplication, where we ask God for help with our specific needs, and intercessory prayers, which focus on lifting up the needs of others. Thanksgiving prayers will remind us to look for blessings even in tough times. At the same time, declarations help us affirm God's promises over our situations. By understanding and utilizing these different forms of prayer, we can strengthen our faith and find solace, no matter what life throws our way.

Understanding the various types of prayers suitable for facing adversity and how they can strengthen faith.

Prayer can be a profound source of strength and hope during challenging times. Let's dive into the types of prayers that are particularly suitable for adversity and how they can help us connect with God on a deeper level.

First, we have prayers of supplication. These are heartfelt pleas where we present our needs to God, asking for His help and intervention. When life's burdens become too heavy, supplication allows us to cast our cares upon Him, trusting that He hears and will respond.

Next, intercessory prayers involve praying on behalf of

others. This selfless act aligns us with God's heart for humanity. By lifting up the struggles and needs of friends, family, or even strangers, we extend God's love and grace into their lives.

Thanksgiving prayers are a powerful way to shift focus from our troubles to gratitude. Even in difficult seasons, acknowledging God's blessings fosters a spirit of thankfulness and reminds us of His faithfulness. It's about finding joy in small victories and maintaining a perspective of hope.

Lastly, declarations are prayers that affirm God's promises and truths over our situations. Speaking life and victory into our circumstances reinforces our faith and trust in God's power. Declarations can transform our mindset, making us more resilient against life's storms.

It's important to be specific in our prayer requests. Clearly articulating our needs helps us communicate more effectively with God. Here is what you can do:

- Identify the exact issues or concerns you're facing.

- Frame your request in a detailed manner.

- Regularly review and update your prayers as situations evolve.

- Persist in bringing these specific needs before God until you see His hand move.

Faith is crucial in believing for breakthroughs and miracles through prayer. It's about having confidence that God is able and willing to intervene. Faith ignites our prayers, turning them from mere words into powerful petitions. Here are steps to cultivate this belief:

- Reflect on past instances where God has answered prayers.
- Immerse yourself in scriptures that reinforce God's promises.
- Surround yourself with testimonies of answered prayers to boost your confidence.
- Continuously surrender your doubts and fears, trusting God's timing and methods.

Consistent prayer helps deepen our intimacy with God and strengthens our reliance on His guidance. It's not just about seeking answers but also about building a relationship. Here's how to maintain consistency:

- Set aside dedicated time each day for prayer.
- Keep a journal to document your conversations with God and reflect on His responses.
- Engage in different forms of prayer to keep your practice dynamic and fresh.

- Involve God in your daily routine, turning every moment into an opportunity for connection.

We also find ourselves more attuned to God's voice and direction through consistent prayer. The more we pray, the more we recognize His guidance in our lives. This practice nurtures a stronger reliance on Him, especially when navigating tough times.

Aligning our prayers with the specific challenges we face is key. By directly addressing the unique aspects of our struggles, we invite God into those precise areas of our lives. Approaching God with faith and persistence ensures we remain steadfast, even when answers seem delayed. It's about trusting that every prayer moves us closer to divine intervention.

In conclusion, understanding and utilizing various types of prayers during adversity equips us with the tools to face life's challenges head-on. By being specific, exercising faith, and remaining consistent, we deepen our relationship with God and position ourselves to witness His miraculous work.

Recognizing the importance of fellowship prayer and its impact on spiritual growth and support.

When life's challenges seem overwhelming, harnessing the transformative power of prayer can be a lifeline. One significant aspect of prayer is its communal nature. The Bible highlights the importance of corporate prayer, emphasizing the strength believers find in unity. This collective approach to prayer isn't just a ritual; it's a source of immense support and spiritual reinforcement.

Throughout the scriptures, we witness remarkable instances where group prayers led to miraculous breakthroughs. In the early church, as depicted in Acts 2:42, the disciples dedicated themselves to the apostles' teaching, fellowship, breaking of bread, and prayer. This devotion wasn't merely about tradition; it was the glue that bound them together as they navigated the immense task of spreading the Gospel.

Take, for example, the moment in Acts 4:31 when believers gathered to pray, and their place of gathering was shaken, filled with the Holy Spirit. This divine encounter emboldened them to speak God's word with tremendous courage. As seen here, group prayer provided not only boldness but also a sense of unity and purpose during times of persecution.

Similarly, in Acts 6:3-4, the early church leaders prioritized prayer alongside their ministry duties, acknowledging its crucial role in guiding their decisions and actions. These biblical narratives illustrate that group prayer has been essential since the church's earliest days, fostering a sense of community and shared mission.

For us today, the principle remains the same. Praying with

others brings about a sense of solidarity and collective power that can be profoundly comforting and empowering during difficult seasons. (What is the importance and value of group prayer? GotQuestions.org., n.d.)

Encouraging readers to seek out prayer partners or join prayer groups can be important for mutual growth and strength. Here is what you can do to experience the full benefits of communal prayer:

- Find like-minded individuals who share your faith and commitment to prayer.

- Create or join a prayer group where you can meet regularly to pray together.

- Foster an environment of openness and trust where everyone feels comfortable sharing their needs and victories.

- Commit to supporting each other through consistent and intentional prayer, reinforcing each other's faith and resilience.

The power of agreement in prayer cannot be overstated. Jesus Himself taught that where two or three are gathered in His name, He is there among them (Matthew 18:20). When believers come together to pray in agreement, it amplifies their petitions, creating a unified front against adversity. This collective effort

75

doesn't just multiply the prayers; it strengthens the individual member's faith, reminding them that they're not alone in their struggles.

Knowing that others are standing with you in prayer during tough times can be incredibly reassuring. It reinforces the idea that while personal responsibility is vital, having a safety net of supportive prayer partners can make a significant difference. Communal prayer allows for bearing each other's burdens, lightening the load, and providing much-needed emotional and spiritual support.

Moreover, there's something uniquely powerful about experiencing answered prayers within a group. Witnessing how God's responses unfold collectively can serve as tangible proof of His working in our lives, thereby deepening our faith and encouraging us to keep pressing forward. This shared journey of prayer brings about individual growth and strengthens the community's bonds.

In conclusion, embracing the practice of praying with others enriches our spiritual lives in multiple ways. It builds a sense of unity, provides strength in adversity, and fosters an environment where God's presence is palpably experienced. Through communal prayer, we find solidarity, encouragement, and a deeper connection with both God and fellow believers, reshaping our approach to life's challenges with hope and resilience.

Remember, joining hands in prayer with others isn't just about seeking divine intervention—it's about building a robust support system that uplifts each member, reinforcing the foundational belief that together, in faith and prayer, we are stronger.

Powerful prayers in the Bible.

Harnessing the transformative power of prayer during challenging seasons can be a powerful practice, especially when we take inspiration from the Bible. Let's dive into some pivotal prayers from notable biblical figures to understand their faith and how they faced their struggles with divine help.

In the Bible, we find many examples of powerful prayers that brought about significant change. Take Abraham, whose prayers were filled with trust in God's promises. When he pleaded for Sodom, his persistence showed his deep concern for others (Genesis 18:22-33). Then there's Hannah, who poured her heart out to God for a child, promising to dedicate him to the Lord's service. Her honest and fervent prayer was answered with the birth of Samuel (1 Samuel 1:10-20) (God Answers Hannah's Prayer. Mission Bible Class., 2011).

David's prayers often reflected his unwavering faith and his reliance on God for deliverance. His psalms are full of praise, repentance, and declarations of God's greatness. Jesus' prayers, especially in Gethsemane, exemplify total surrender to God's will even amid immense suffering (Matthew 26:36-42). These prayers succeeded because of key elements like trust in God's promises, complete surrender to His will, and perseverance.

We can draw parallels between the situations faced by these biblical characters and our own struggles. Abraham's concern for Sodom reflects our concerns for justice today. Hannah's deep longing and emotional honesty can resonate with anyone facing infertility or deep personal grief. David's pleas for protection against enemies can mirror our cries for help against adversities in life. Jesus' prayer in Gethsemane teaches us the power of submission to God's plan, even when it leads us through pain.

Encouraging readers to pattern their prayers after these biblical models can be incredibly beneficial.

Here's what you can do:

- Start by expressing praise and adoration towards God.

- Include thanksgiving, recounting past blessings, and answered prayers.

- Make faith declarations, stating your trust in God's promises.

- Be specific about your requests, laying out your needs clearly before God.

These steps enhance the effectiveness of your prayers and deepen your relationship with God. Incorporating these elements helps create a balanced prayer life that aligns with biblical examples.

By examining these prayers and their components, readers can gain timeless lessons on prayer's power. The faith-filled prayers of Abraham, Hannah, David, and Jesus reveal that trusting in God's promises, surrendering fully to His will, and persevering in seeking Him are integral to effective prayer.

Reflecting on these examples, we find that trusting in God's promises builds a foundation of hope and assurance. Surrendering to His will aligns our desires with His divine plan, opening the door for His perfect work in our lives. Perseverance ensures that we stay connected to God, continually seeking His guidance and support, no matter how long the wait may be.

These biblical heroes' faith-filled prayers will inspire readers. They provide a template for crafting our own prayers, infusing them with praise, gratitude, and declarations of faith. By following these models, we can confidently approach God, knowing He hears and responds to our heartfelt prayers.

Incorporating elements from these prayers into your own can lead to breakthroughs and incredible resilience in challenging times.

After all, prayer is not just about asking for things; it's about building a robust relationship with God that stands firm in the face of adversity. By learning from Abraham's intercessory prayers, Hannah's earnest petitions, David's psalms of praise and repentance, and Jesus' ultimate act of surrender, we can develop a prayer life that is both powerful and transformative.

Ultimately, the key takeaway is that through prayer, we tap into divine strength and wisdom, gaining the endurance to navigate life's toughest seasons. By looking to the examples set by biblical figures, we can craft prayers that are heartfelt, grounded in trust, and filled with faith, thus enabling us to experience the profound peace and assurance that comes from connecting deeply with God.

Testimonies of answered prayers.

Harnessing the transformative power of prayer during challenging seasons can profoundly impact our lives. Real-life testimonies of answered prayers often serve as a beacon of hope and encouragement, reinforcing our faith in God's faithfulness and intervention.

Take, for instance, Sherry King's story shared in Guideposts—a woman awaiting a cancer diagnosis found solace through prayer. As she poured her heart into God, she experienced an overwhelming sense of peace that enveloped her like a blanket. This comfort was not just an emotional reaction but a tangible manifestation of divine intervention in her time of need (True Prayers Answered Stories).

(Archives. Guideposts., n.d.).

Another inspiring account comes from Cathy Henn, who felt alone while attending an overcrowded mass. Despite being outside the barn, her prayer led to a poignant realization that she wasn't truly alone. She felt a divine presence standing with her, reminding us that sometimes, God's answers come through subtle reassurances rather than grand gestures (True (Prayers Answered Stories Archives. Guideposts., n.d.).

These testimonies highlight various ways people have experienced God's faithfulness—through healing, provision, or guidance. For example, Roberta Messner's unexpected blessing came in the form of a new friendship when she prayed for help in purchasing a bedroom set. Her story emphasizes how God can provide exactly what we need, even if it isn't precisely what we asked for (True Prayers Answered Stories Archives. Guideposts., n.d.).

Faith, persistence, and expectancy are critical in witnessing God's miraculous work in response to heartfelt prayers. Here is what you can do to achieve this:

- Approach each prayer with unwavering faith, believing wholeheartedly in God's ability and willingness to respond.

- Persist in your prayers, even when the answer seems delayed. Continuously reaching out to God demonstrates trust and reliance on His timing.

- Maintain a spirit of expectancy, looking forward to how God manifests His power and grace in your situation.

An essential aspect of effective prayer is reflecting on personal experiences of answered prayers. Reflecting on past instances where God has intervened can strengthen your resolve and encourage steadfastness in faith.

One compelling story is about Rick Hamlin, whose family and church community rallied in prayer for his mother during her battle with COVID-19. Their collective prayers resulted in her miraculous recovery, showcasing the power of united supplication and the importance of faith within a supportive community (True Prayers Answered. Stories Archives. Guideposts., n.d.).

Encourage yourself by recounting your own experiences where prayer changed the course of events in your life. This reflection nurtures a deep-seated trust in God's faithfulness and encourages continuous reliance on Him.

Here is what you can do to remain steadfast in your trust in God's faithfulness:

- Regularly document your prayers and their outcomes. This practice helps you see patterns of God's responses over time.

- Share your testimonies with others. Speaking about God's interventions encourages those around you and reinforces your faith.

- Surround yourself with a community that values prayer. Engaging with others who share similar beliefs can bolster your confidence and perseverance.

Testimonies are powerful. They bring abstract concepts like faith and divine intervention into the realm of reality. By sharing these stories, we uplift one another and remind ourselves of the power inherent in a life anchored by prayer.

In times of trial, it's easy to feel isolated or abandoned. However, these stories collectively tell us otherwise. They echo a consistent message of God's unwavering presence and responsiveness. When facing personal challenges, whether large or small, remember that prayer can be the conduit through which divine assistance flows.

To conclude, the transformative power of prayer lies not just in the act itself but in the faith, persistence, and expectancy with which we approach it. By continually seeking God's face, trusting in His timing, and expecting His intervention, we open ourselves to witnessing His miraculous work in our lives. Embrace the journey, reflect on past victories, and remain steadfast. God's faithfulness endures through all seasons.

Key Takeaways.

We've explored how different types of prayer can transform challenging seasons and deepen our relationship with God. From supplication to intercessory prayers, thanksgiving to declarations, each type offers a unique way to connect with Him and face adversity head-on.

Remember when we talked about the power of being specific in our requests to God? That still holds true. Articulating our needs clearly helps us communicate better with Him and trust that He's listening and will respond. Faith is key here believing in God's ability to intervene turns our words into powerful petitions. This kind of faith isn't just a fleeting thought; it requires reflection on past answered prayers, diving into scripture, and surrounding ourselves with stories of God's work.

Then, there's the idea of praying consistently. It's not only about seeking answers but also about growing closer to God. Setting aside time each day, keeping a prayer journal, and making every moment an opportunity for connection can help maintain this consistency. Regular prayer makes us more attuned to God's voice and direction, which is crucial when life's storms hit hard.

The persistence required, especially when answers seem delayed, might be concerning for some. It can be tough to keep praying without seeing immediate results. But remember, every prayer moves us closer to divine intervention, even if it doesn't feel like it at the moment. This persistence builds resilience, helping us endure until we witness God's miraculous work.

On a broader scale, these practices transform individual lives and strengthen communities. Sharing testimonies of answered prayers fosters collective hope and faith. When people come together to pray, they form a unified front against adversity, creating a support system that uplifts everyone involved.

So, as you navigate your challenges, think about how to incorporate these kinds of prayers into your life. Be specific, have faith, stay consistent, and don't hesitate to lean on others for support. Remember, prayer is a journey that deepens our bond with God and equips us with the strength to face whatever comes our way. Let's continue to harness the power of prayer, trusting that it's shaping us and bringing us closer to His incredible plan for our lives.

Chapter Six.

Renewing Hope and Vision

Imagine standing in the middle of a stormy sea. Waves crash loudly around you, and the wind fiercely pushes against you. It's easy to feel small and defenseless in such a situation. But what if you had the power to speak to those waves and command them to be still? This is not just a fantasy; it's the kind of authority that believers have been given through Christ. Recognizing and using this spiritual authority can transform how you face life's toughest storms.

Life throws all kinds of challenges at us health problems, financial issues, and emotional struggles. For instance, Sarah faced a daunting health diagnosis that seemed impossible to overcome. Despite the severity of her condition, she clung to the belief that she had spiritual authority through Christ. Every day, she proclaimed healing over her body. Similarly, Mark battled crippling financial instability but steadfastly declared God's provision over his life. Over time, both saw remarkable changes in their situations, showing that spiritual authority can turn the tide in seemingly hopeless scenarios.

In this chapter, we're diving into how to tap into this incredible resource. We'll explore spiritual authority and provide practical steps to wield it effectively. From speaking words of victory over your obstacles to praying with total confidence, you'll learn how to stand firm in your faith. By internalizing these principles, you'll be equipped to face any storm that comes your way, firmly believing that you can overcome it through the power given to you by Christ.

Understanding Spiritual Authority

Understanding Spiritual Authority

Exploring the concept of spiritual authority granted by Christ is essential for believers striving to navigate life's storms. Many people see challenges as impossible, but understanding the spiritual authority given by Christ can transform that perspective. This authority empowers us to approach trials with confidence and faith. When you recognize the power within you, it becomes a game-changer.

The spiritual authority extends beyond our visible realm into a spiritual one, impacting our circumstances profoundly. It's like having a toolkit that's been there all along, just waiting to be used. With this authority, believers can declare victory and break through obstacles in challenging times. How do you harness this authority? Here are some practical steps:

- Start by believing and accepting that you have this authority through Christ.
- Speak words of victory over your challenges, declaring outcomes aligned with God's promises.
- Stay consistent in your declarations, even when situations seem unchanged.
- Pray with authority, commanding barriers to move and doors to open.

Operate in Faith with Authority

Faith and authority are deeply interconnected when invoking God's power during adversity. To operate effectively in your spiritual authority, it's crucial to strengthen your faith. Exercising spiritual authority in prayers and declarations can be a powerful practice. Here's how to make the most of it:

- Engage in daily prayer, asking God for strength and guidance.
- Declare scriptures over your life that reinforce victory and authority.
- Visualize the positive changes you're praying for, firmly believing they will manifest.

Applying biblical principles helps assert authority over negative situations. Speak life into them by using scriptures that promise hope and deliverance.

Cultivating a mindset of victory starts with understanding and applying these principles consistently.

Claiming Victory in Christ

Realizing that spiritual authority is not just a concept but a powerful tool for transforming circumstances is key. You can claim victory over life's storms through this authority as a believer. Here are some guidelines to help you:

- Recognize your identity as a child of God, which gives you inherent authority.
- Overcome fear and doubt by consistently reminding yourself of God's promises.
- Stand firm on these promises, proclaiming them with boldness to see breakthroughs.

When faced with adversity, it's easy to feel defeated. But remember that you are equipped with spiritual authority to overcome every storm. This isn't about ignoring reality but engaging with it from a position of strength and trust in God's power.

Every declaration made in faith shifts the atmosphere around you. You're not just speaking words; you're engaging in spiritual warfare that pushes back against the forces trying to bring you down.

Harnessing Spiritual Authority to Declare Victory

Declaring victory isn't just wishful thinking; it's an active engagement in the spiritual battle. You can command situations to align with divine purposes by harnessing your spiritual authority.

Here's how:

- Dedicate time each day for specific declarations of faith.
- Focus on areas where you seek change, stating clearly what you want to happen.
- Use scriptural backing to give weight to your declarations, aligning them with God's word.

For instance, if you're facing financial struggles, declare that God will provide for all your needs according to His riches in glory. If it's a health issue, speak healing over your body, referencing scriptures that promise health and wholeness.

Operate in Faith with Authority

Having faith is crucial when exercising spiritual authority. It's the foundation upon which your declarations stand. Strengthening your faith involves both speaking and hearing the word of God regularly.

Here's a guideline to follow:

- Read faith-building scriptures daily to keep your spirit strong.
- Surround yourself with positive affirmations and testimonies.
- Attend gatherings or listen to teachings that reinforce your understanding of spiritual authority.

Applying biblical principles to assert authority over negative situations requires a proactive approach. Don't wait until things go wrong to start declaring victory. Make it a part of your daily routine, ensuring your faith remains strong no matter what challenges arise.

Cultivating a Mindset of Victory

A victorious mindset doesn't come overnight but is developed through regular practice and the application of spiritual principles. Understanding and applying spiritual authority should become second nature.

Take steps like:

- Regularly reflecting on past victories and how God brought you through.
- Journaling your prayers and declarations to track progress and build confidence.

- Engaging in faith-filled conversations that inspire and uplift you.

Overcoming Fear and Doubt

Fear and doubt can undermine your spiritual authority. Stepping into your identity as a child of God means embracing the full spectrum of the authority bestowed upon you. Whenever fear creeps in, counter it with declarations of faith. Remember, God has not given you a spirit of fear but of power, love, and a sound mind.

Standing Firm on God's Promises

Standing firm on God's promises requires knowing those promises well. Spend time in scripture, internalizing the truths reinforcing your authority in Christ. Proclaim these promises boldly, especially when your circumstances challenge them.

Consistency is key don't waver in your declarations

In conclusion, using the authority given by Christ empowers you to face life's storms with confidence. It's about understanding who you are in Him, harnessing that power through faith-filled declarations, and standing unwaveringly on His promises. By doing so, you'll not only navigate challenges but emerge victorious.

Speaking Life and Truth

Using the authority given by Christ to overcome life's storms can be an empowering and transformative journey. To fully embrace this authority, we need actionable steps that strengthen our spiritual discernment and enable us to navigate challenges effectively.

Speaking Life and Truth

Our words have power. They shape our reality and influence our outcomes. Speaking life and truth means using our words to align with God's promises and declare positive change in challenging situations.

- Begin by reflecting on your current struggles. Identify specific areas where you need transformation.
- Find biblical truths and promises related to those areas. Write them down and meditate on them daily.
- Speak these truths aloud. Make declarations over your life that affirm what God has promised you.
- Surround yourself with people who encourage and speak life into your circumstances.

Harnessing the authority in Christ is about more than just positive thinking; it's about anchoring your words in His eternal truth. Declare victory over obstacles through the power Christ has given you.

Practicing Affirmations Rooted in Biblical Truth

Affirmations are powerful when they are rooted in Scripture. They help shift our perspectives and align our thoughts with God's will.

- Daily affirmations should reflect God's promises. For instance, "I am more than a conqueror through Him who loves me" (Romans 8:37).
- Consistency is key. Practice these affirmations daily to start your day with a positive and hopeful mindset.
- Encourage others by sharing your affirmations. This not only reinforces your belief but also builds a supportive community.

By integrating biblical truth into our affirmations, we foster personal growth and strengthen our faith in God's plans for us.

Understanding the Impact of Speaking Positively

Speaking positively isn't just about optimism; it's about aligning our speech with God's promises. When faced with trials, declaring God's truth can change the atmosphere and open doors for breakthroughs. When we consistently speak words affirming God's goodness and faithfulness, we position ourselves to see His hand at work.

Developing Spiritual Discernment

Spiritual discernment is crucial for recognizing God's leading and making wise decisions. Here's how you can develop it:

- Regularly engage in prayer and meditation. This sharpens your spiritual senses and helps you hear God's voice more clearly.
- Train your spirit through consistent spiritual disciplines like reading the Bible, fasting, and worship.
- Learn to distinguish between truth and deception. Regularly ask God for wisdom and insight into various situations.

Training in spiritual discernment equips us to face life's storms with confidence and clarity, knowing that we're guided by divine wisdom.

Engaging in Prayer and Meditation

Prayer and meditation are vital practices for enhancing spiritual discernment. They quiet the noise around us and tune our hearts to God's frequency.

- Set aside dedicated time each day for prayer and meditation. Even a few minutes can make a significant difference.
- Use Scripture as a foundation for your meditation. Ponder its meaning and ask God to reveal deeper insights.

- Maintain a journal to record your prayers, reflections, and any discernments you receive. This helps track your spiritual growth and God's responses.

Training the Spirit Through Regular Spiritual Disciplines

Spiritual disciplines keep us grounded and spiritually alert. They build resilience and enhance our ability to discern God's voice amidst life's chaos.

- Commit to daily Bible reading. Choose a reading plan that suits your schedule and stick with it.
- Engage in regular fasting. It's a powerful way to humble yourself and seek God's guidance.
- Be part of a faith community. Sharing experiences and learning from others strengthens your spiritual journey.

Regular spiritual disciplines fortify us, enabling us to stand firm against negative influences and deceptive tactics.

Providing Tools for Distinguishing Spiritual Warfare

Spiritual warfare requires discernment and the right tools to combat negative influences effectively.

- Equip yourself with Scripture. Memorize verses that address spiritual battles and use them in prayer.
- Practice binding and losing prayers. Bind negative spirits and lose God's peace, love, and truth over your situation.

- Partner with others in prayer. A united front in prayer can break strongholds and bring about significant victories.

Knowing how to recognize and respond to spiritual warfare empowers us to apply Christ's authority decisively.

As we navigate life's storms, it's essential to maintain a proactive approach toward utilizing spiritual authority. By speaking life-affirming declarations, practicing biblical affirmations, and developing spiritual discernment, we can effectively harness the authority given by Christ. These steps guide us through challenges and deepen our relationship with God, ensuring that we emerge stronger and more resilient.

Exercises for Developing Spiritual Discernment

Life's storms can hit us hard and unexpectedly, leaving us feeling helpless. Yet, through the authority given by Christ, we can find strength to overcome these challenges. Seeing how real-life examples showcase the victories achieved through spiritual authority is inspiring.

To develop spiritual discernment, practical exercises are essential. Start by engaging in guided prayer exercises. Spend time in quiet reflection, asking God for clarity and guidance. These moments of stillness can deepen your connection with God and help you recognize His voice amidst life's chaos.

Journaling is another valuable tool. Reflecting on personal experiences can reveal patterns where spiritual authority played a role. Write about times when faith-filled words brought peace or solutions to troubling situations. This practice boosts your discernment and strengthens your faith as you recount God's work in your life.

Group activities offer collective growth in discerning spiritual influences. Gather with others to discuss and pray over specific challenges, sharing insights and supporting each other. Practicing discernment together enhances your ability to identify spiritual truths and provides a strong support network.

Real-life victories through spiritual authority abound, illustrating its transformational power. Take, for instance, Sarah's story. Faced with a health crisis, she embraced her spiritual authority, declaring healing over herself daily. Over time, her faith-inspired declarations resulted in a remarkable recovery, defying medical expectations.

Another powerful narrative is Mark's. Struggling with financial instability, he harnessed his spiritual authority by proclaiming God's provision. His consistent declarations, grounded in faith, led to unexpected job opportunities and financial stability. These stories demonstrate that active engagement with spiritual authority can lead to tangible, victorious outcomes.

Let's look at practical applications. When facing adversity, remind yourself of the authority you hold in Christ. Speak out positive affirmations and biblical promises about your situation. For example, if you're battling anxiety, declare scriptures like, "God has not given me a spirit of fear, but of power, love, and a sound mind" (2 Timothy 1:7). Repeatedly speaking these truths can shift your mindset and circumstances.

Group activities can further reinforce this practice. In small gatherings, share scriptures and speak them collectively over shared concerns. This collective declaration not only builds faith but also strengthens community bonds.

Testimonies of breakthroughs often involve faith-filled declarations. Jane's story of overcoming depression illustrates this well. She consistently declared, "The joy of the Lord is my strength" (Nehemiah 8:10), even when she didn't feel it. Gradually, her mindset shifted, and she experienced a profound emotional breakthrough. Such testimonies highlight the practical application of spiritual authority in real-world scenarios.

In conclusion, life's storms are inevitable, but with the authority given by Christ, we can face them head-on. We develop the spiritual discernment needed to navigate challenges through guided prayer, journaling, group activities, and faith-filled declarations. Real-life victories remind us that spiritual authority is a powerful tool to transform our circumstances. By embracing this authority, we step into a place of victory and witness the incredible outcomes God has in store for us.

Key Takeaways.

Throughout this chapter, we've explored the profound concept of spiritual authority Christ gives and its power to help us overcome life's storms. We began by understanding that many of us view challenges as insurmountable, but recognizing and harnessing this authority can transform our perspective, allowing us to face trials with confidence and faith.

At the start, we discussed the importance of believing in and accepting this authority. This foundational step sets the stage for approaching life's challenges from a position of strength. Speaking words of victory, staying consistent in our declarations, and praying with authority are practical ways to exercise this power.

Faith plays a vital role in exercising spiritual authority. It's not enough to know we have this authority; we must also strengthen our faith through daily practices such as prayer, declaring scriptures, and visualizing positive outcomes. By doing so, we align ourselves more closely with God's promises, helping us assert authority over negative situations effectively.

Realizing our identity as children of God reinforces our inherent authority and helps us overcome fear and doubt. When adversity strikes, it's essential to remember that we're equipped with spiritual authority to declare victory. This is not about ignoring reality but engaging it from a place of faith and trust in God's power.

Using our spiritual authority involves actively commanding situations to align with divine purposes. Dedicating time for specific declarations and using scriptural backing gives weight to our words, ensuring they align with God's truth. Consistency is key. Making these declarations part of our daily routine helps us maintain strong faith no matter what challenges arise.

Overcoming fear and doubt is another crucial aspect. We stand firm on God's promises by countering negative thoughts with declarations of faith. Spending time in scripture, internalizing truths, and proclaiming them boldly help us stay grounded.

In conclusion, the authority given by Christ empowers us to face life's storms confidently. It's about knowing who we are in Him, making faith-filled declarations, and standing unwaveringly on His promises. By embracing this authority, we navigate challenges and emerge victorious, experiencing the transformative power of faith in every aspect of our lives. Let's continue to speak life and truth, practice biblical affirmations, and develop spiritual discernment to harness Christ's authority for lasting change fully.

Chapter Seven.

Community Support and Accountability

Have you ever faced a tough time and felt like you were tackling it alone? It's easy to feel overwhelmed when challenges pile up, but the power of community can make all the difference. Small groups and fellowship provide a lifeline through life's storms, offering support, encouragement, and a sense of belonging that we all need. When we come together in these intimate settings, we build bonds that help us share burdens and celebrate victories, strengthening our resilience.

The problem many face, though, is trying to go it alone. We might think we should handle everything ourselves or fear being judged if we open up about our struggles. But, this self-reliance can lead to isolation and burnout. For instance, those who attend small group meetings regularly often find they handle stress better because they aren't bearing their troubles solo. Sharing experiences and praying with others can lift spirits and lighten loads. The Bible even shows us the importance of bearing each other's burdens, as seen in the early church's communal living and mutual support.

This chapter let's dive e into how leveraging community support and accountability can help navigate tough times. We'll explore the essential role of small groups and fellowship in boosting faith and resilience. You'll discover practical steps for creating and maintaining strong small group dynamics and how engaging in fellowship can transform your journey. Through examples and actionable tips, we'll see how sharing personal stories within a supportive community can foster growth and enduring strength. So, get ready to learn how to harness the power of community to weather any storm that comes your way!

Exploring the role of small groups and fellowship in strengthening one's faith and resilience during challenging times.

Leveraging community support and accountability to navigate storms is crucial for personal growth and resilience. One of the fundamental aspects is the role that small groups play. Small groups provide an intimate space where individuals can develop meaningful relationships, offer mutual support, and engage in collective prayer. These environments foster a sense of belonging and encouragement during challenging times. When people come together in small groups, they create a platform for sharing their struggles, victories, and prayers, reinforcing a culture of unity and shared burdens.

To effectively leverage the power of small groups, here are some guidelines:

- Make it a habit to attend regular meetings and commit to being present in both good and difficult times.
- Share openly and honestly about your challenges and successes, creating a safe space for others to do the same.
- Actively listen and provide constructive feedback and encouragement to group members.
- Set personal and group goals and hold each other accountable for progress through regular check-ins.
- Engage in collective prayer, focusing on specific needs and intentions within the group.

Small group dynamics are essential for personal growth. Individuals enhance their spiritual maturity and resilience through shared experiences, diverse perspectives, and collaborative learning. Engaging in group activities and discussions deepens connections, builds trust, and promotes authentic fellowship that sustains individuals during adversity.

Fellowship plays a vital role in navigating life's storms. The Bible provides powerful examples of communal support during troublesome times, highlighting the significance of bearing one another's burdens and uplifting each other through prayer and good deeds. Fellowship creates an environment filled with love, empathy, and compassion, enabling individuals to find solace, wisdom, and practical help within a caring community.

Participating in fellowship activities like group studies, communal worship, and service projects fosters unity, resilience, and mutual edification. These activities strengthen individuals to face daunting challenges with faith and courage. To actively engage in fellowship:

- Join or form study groups to explore and discuss biblical teachings, drawing strength from collective learning.
- Participate in communal worship activities in person or virtually to maintain a connection with your faith community.
- Volunteer for service projects that address the community's immediate needs, reinforcing a sense of purpose and solidarity.

The value of sharing personal struggles and triumphs within a supportive community cannot be overstated. Doing so alleviates feelings of loneliness and isolation while bolstering faith, hope, and perseverance through shared testimonies of God's faithfulness. Sharing not only strengthens individual resolve but also fosters a stronger communal bond.

Here is how you can share effectively within your community:

- Be vulnerable and transparent about your experiences to inspire others and build deeper connections.
- Encourage others to share their stories and listen actively, providing empathy and understanding.
- Celebrate collective and individual achievements as a community, reinforcing positive reinforcement and communal joy.
- Use shared testimonies to reflect on God's faithfulness and build a culture of gratitude and acknowledgment.

In conclusion, engaging in small groups and fellowship activities is key to navigating life's storms. These environments foster genuine connections, mutual support, and spiritual growth, providing the strength needed to overcome adversities. Individuals can build resilient communities grounded in collective faith and support by participating in small groups, committing to fellowship, and sharing personal stories.

Understanding the importance of developing accountability partnerships for spiritual growth and endurance.

Leveraging community support and accountability to navigate life's storms is key to creating a resilient and empowered path forward. Establishing accountability partnerships involves committing to mutual encouragement, honesty, and discernment. This fosters growth, maturity, and resilience in one's spiritual journey. Transparency, vulnerability, and accountability in areas of personal struggles, temptations, and spiritual disciplines can lead to significant growth, freedom, and empowerment in overcoming challenges.

Here is what you can do to achieve this:

- Find someone you trust deeply.
- Be open about your struggles and successes.
- Set shared goals that promote spiritual growth.
- Regularly check in and pray for one another.

Partnering with a trusted individual for accountability builds trust and loyalty, creating a safe space for confession, repentance, and support. This nurturing environment fosters a culture of grace and restoration during times of vulnerability and failure. Regular check-ins, shared goals, and prayerful support within these relationships offer a framework for mutual growth, trust-building, and intentional progress toward spiritual maturity and victory.

Understanding the transformative power of accountability is crucial. When we allow others to see our struggles and support us, we can gain insights into ourselves that might otherwise go unnoticed. Accountability helps us refocus our spiritual awareness and even boosts our physical energy by encouraging breaks and proper boundaries (Understanding and Developing Christian Accountability. Churchleadership.org., 2024).

In accountability dynamics, focusing on mutual encouragement rather than just addressing shortcomings is essential. It's about building each other up. For instance, having an accountability partner who checks in on your daily prayer habit can help maintain consistency. Additionally, this partnership provides a sounding board for advice and feedback, guiding both parties toward more fruitful spiritual practices.

Furthermore, accountability isn't limited to monitoring behavior; it's about achieving goals and celebrating milestones together (4 Reasons Accountability Is Invaluable in the Christian Life Jesus Film Project, 2021). An accountability partner can help set realistic, actionable goals, whether it's reading a chapter of the Bible each day or spending a specific amount of time in prayer. They provide the encouragement needed to stay committed and the joy of shared victories.

It's also vital to avoid burnout through proper accountability. Burnout can happen when our spiritual energies are exhausted. With an accountability partner, we have someone to remind us to take care of our well-being, set necessary boundaries, and take time to rest. This support can prevent the feeling of isolation and encourage perseverance in faith.

Having regular check-ins fosters a culture of intentional growth. These moments aren't just for discussing failures but planning for success. By sharing our plans and expectations, we create a support system that nurtures continual improvement. This structure facilitates growth in both individuals and the community, ensuring that progress is celebrated and setbacks are tackled collectively.

An essential part of accountability is the culture of confession and forgiveness. Feeling free to admit mistakes without fear of judgment cultivates a therapeutic environment. It's about recognizing our flaws and finding ways to overcome them with the help of compassionate partners who are equally invested in our spiritual growth.

Moreover, having an accountability partner helps maintain enthusiasm and engagement in our faith journey. Shared passion in serving the Lord energizes and keeps us anchored to our spiritual commitments.

Surrounding ourselves with like-minded individuals who share our enthusiasm makes maintaining zeal easier, especially in challenging times. Their fire becomes ours when our own dwindles.

Choosing the right accountability partner is crucial.

Seek out those who share your values and commitment to spiritual growth. A good partner will not only share their own struggles and triumphs but also respect yours. This mutual respect forms the bedrock of a productive and empowering relationship where both can grow and thrive spiritually.

To sum up, leveraging community support and accountability offers a powerful means to navigate life's storms. By committing to mutual encouragement, transparency, and consistent support, we can foster an environment where spiritual growth flourishes. This balanced approach helps individuals overcome personal challenges and strengthens the fabric of the entire community, leading to collective victory in the pursuit of faith and resilience.

Establishing a scriptural foundation for communal support and its significance in navigating life's storms.

One of the most compelling examples of leveraging community support and accountability comes from the early Church, described vividly in Acts. This group of believers was wholly devoted to fellowship, prayer, and mutual support, creating a unity that helped them navigate various trials and tribulations. They shared their lives, resources, and faith, experiencing significant spiritual power that saw them through times of adversity.

In Acts 2:42-47, we see a tightly-knit church committed to several practices. They devoted themselves to the apostles' teaching, fellowship, breaking bread, and prayer. Their deep connections meant no one was in need because they deeply cared for each other. This wasn't just about sharing resources but about living out Jesus' command to love one another earnestly. They broke bread together in homes, emphasizing smaller groups within the larger community, which fostered intimate and meaningful relationships. The power of God was evident in many signs and wonders performed by the apostles, filling everyone with awe. This miraculous nature became a hallmark of their testimony and communal life. (Community - Acts 2:42-47.

Redeemer Anglican Church., 2020).

Paul's letters often highlight this interconnectedness in the body of Christ. He underscores the need for encouragement, edification, and accountability within a community supporting each other in faith and love. For instance, Paul's counsel to the Thessalonians emphasizes encouraging one another and building up each other, as they were already doing. Such guidance is essential for creating a robust community where every member feels supported and valued.

Another perspective on community support and its significance comes from Proverbs and Ecclesiastes. These books offer wisdom about companionship, seeking wise counsel, and sharing burdens. Proverbs 27:17 states, "As iron sharpens iron, so one person sharpens another," illustrating that wise and honest friendships enhance our character and decision-making abilities. In Ecclesiastes 4:9-10, we read, "Two are better than one because they have a good return for their labor: If either of them falls down, one can help the other up." This passage reflects the strength and protection found in supportive communities, where members look out for each other's well-being.

Scripture is also rich with promises assuring believers of God's presence and provision within a faith community. Matthew 18:20 reminds us, "where two or three gather in my name, there am

I with them." This promise shows the transformative power of communal unity and prayer in overcoming life's challenges. When we gather in faith and love, whether for prayer, support, or fellowship, we invite God's presence into our midst, ensuring His guidance and strength.

The Bible affirms that God honors prayers and agreements made in unity, leading to breakthroughs and miracles that glorify His name. James 5:16 encourages believers to confess their sins to each other and pray for one another so they may be healed, underscoring the importance of mutual support rooted in faith.

To truly harness the power of community in navigating life's storms, we can learn from these biblical principles:

- **Commit to Fellowship:** Engage actively in your community by joining regular gatherings in large or smaller congregations. Being part of a close-knit group can provide a consistent support system.

- **Share Resources Generously:** Whether it's time, skills, or material goods, share what you have to meet the needs of others. This builds trust and demonstrates the love of Christ in practical ways.

- **Pray Together Frequently:** Make communal prayer a regular practice. Not only does it strengthen your bond with others, but it also invites God's presence and power into your circumstances.

- **Encourage and Build Each Other Up:** Intentionally encourage others and offer constructive feedback. This helps everyone grow spiritually and emotionally.

- **Seek Wise Counsel:** When facing decisions, seek the advice of trusted, wise community members. They can offer insights you might not have considered.

- **Carry Each Other's Burdens:** Be there for others in tough times and allow others to support you when needed. No one should face life's challenges alone.

By integrating these practices into your life, you cultivate a community that supports you and keeps you accountable, aligning with God's design for empathetic and enduring relationships. This balance of economic growth and human welfare, focusing on human welfare mirrors how the early Church thrived amidst adversities through communal support and accountability.

Exploring the delicate balance between self-reliance and community reliance in navigating life's storms with faith and grace.

Navigating life's storms requires both independent faith and interdependent fellowship. Personal faith and reliance on God are essential, but so is the strength found in a supportive community.

Independent Faith: Personal faith entails an individual journey where trust, surrender, and obedience to God's word play key roles. Cultivating a vibrant personal relationship with Him through prayer, studying His word, and worship forms the bedrock of resilient faith. This self-reliance allows believers to discern and grow spiritually, helping them withstand external pressures and opposition by reflecting deep convictions and communion with God. This independence also enables individuals to seek God's will and tap into their unique gifts, contributing authentically to the community while receiving necessary support and correction.

Interdependent Fellowship: Balancing self-reliance with community reliance involves embracing interdependence within the body of Christ. Here, each member's strengths and weaknesses contribute to the overall health and unity of the community. Recognizing this mutual dependence fosters growth, accountability, and resilience as challenges are faced together.

- Embrace the diversity of spiritual gifts within the community.
- Be open to giving and receiving grace, wisdom, and love.
- Acknowledge that each person's experience and perspective enriches the collective journey.

Interdependence in fellowship encourages a culture of honor, humility, and service where grace and wisdom flow freely. This dynamic mirrors the relational nature of God within His people. It emphasizes the beauty and strength found in unity amid diversity, enabling believers to navigate life's storms with freedom, victory, and maturity through Christ's power and grace.

Understanding the balance between personal faith and communal support helps readers see how these elements work together to foster a strong, resilient faith journey.

Key Takeaways

So, we've discussed the importance of community support and accountability in navigating life's storms. Small groups and fellowship play a pivotal role in helping us stay strong and resilient. They provide an intimate space for sharing our struggles and victories, making us feel less alone and more supported.

Remember how we talked about the power of small groups? We create a nurturing environment that promotes spiritual growth and unity by attending regular meetings, being honest about our challenges, listening actively, setting goals, and praying together. It's about building each other up and walking through tough times hand-in-hand.

Then there's fellowship, which is all about the collective strength found in unity. Engaging in group studies, communal worship, and service projects brings us closer to our faith and each other. This connection helps us face difficulties with courage and hope, knowing we have a community that cares.

Sharing personal stories within these groups is incredibly valuable. It reduces feelings of isolation and boosts faith and perseverance. When we are open about our experiences, we inspire others and build deeper connections. Celebrating achievements together creates a sense of joy and gratitude that strengthens our bonds.

Moving on to accountability partnerships they are essential for spiritual growth and endurance. Finding someone you trust, being open about your struggles, setting shared goals, and checking in regularly can significantly impact your journey. These partnerships create a safe space for confession, support, and mutual encouragement.

Accountability isn't just about pointing out flaws; it's about celebrating milestones and encouraging one another. A good partner helps maintain consistency in spiritual practices and provides a sounding board for advice and feedback. This mutual respect and support lead to significant growth and resilience.

Let's not forget the biblical foundation for community

support. The early Church in Acts, Paul's letters, Proverbs, and Ecclesiastes all emphasize the importance of fellowship, sharing resources, prayer, and mutual encouragement. By following these principles, we can cultivate a supportive community that aligns with God's design for empathetic and enduring relationships.

Balancing self-reliance with community reliance is key to navigating life's storms with faith and grace. Personal faith helps us grow individually, while interdependent fellowship allows us to lean on each other during tough times. Embracing this balance fosters a strong, resilient faith journey.

In the end, leveraging community support and accountability offers a powerful way to overcome challenges. Committing to transparency, mutual encouragement, and consistent support creates an environment where spiritual growth flourishes. This approach not only aids individuals but also strengthens the entire community, leading to collective victory in faith and resilience.

What we take away from this chapter is simple yet profound: Together, we are stronger. Navigating life's storms becomes more manageable when we rely on both our personal faith and the support of our community. So, let's continue to build these resilient communities grounded in collective faith and mutual support, ensuring we all thrive in our spiritual journeys.

Chapter Eight.

Living Victoriously Through Persistence

Imagine being able to conquer life's toughest challenges, not by sheer force but through unwavering persistence. Think about those moments when giving up seemed like the easiest option—whether it was in your career, relationships, or personal growth. Now, picture flipping that script, facing each hurdle with a relentless drive fueled by faith. This kind of tenacity can truly transform your life, making you stronger and more resilient.

We all face obstacles that test our resolve. Maybe it's the frustration of seeing others advance while you're stuck in the same place, or the sinking feeling of hitting a dead end after countless efforts. It could be the weight of daily struggles, from financial worries to health issues. Take Sarah, for example, who battled a serious illness, or Jake, who grew up in a tough neighborhood. They both faced overwhelming odds yet found strength in their faith and perseverance. Their stories remind us that setbacks are universal, but

119

how we approach them defines our journey.

In this chapter, we'll explore how to cultivate persistence and resilience by turning to powerful Biblical examples of unwavering faith. You'll learn practical strategies for building spiritual endurance, even in the face of life's many disappointments. From developing a consistent prayer routine to leaning on God's strength, we'll guide you on how to turn every challenge into an opportunity for growth. By the end, you'll see how persistent faith can lead to living victoriously, no matter what comes your way.

Learning from biblical examples.

Let's dive into cultivating persistence and resilience through faith by reflecting on some powerful Biblical examples.

The story of the persistent widow in Luke 18:1-8 is a testament to unwavering determination. She continually approached an unjust judge, pleading for justice against her adversary. Despite his initial reluctance, her constant petitions compelled him to act on her behalf. This narrative illustrates the importance of persistence, even when faced with resistance or indifference. Now, think about the modern challenges you face—whether it's battling through career hurdles, health issues, or personal conflicts. Just like the widow, persistent prayer and faith can make a significant difference.

Another striking example is the Canaanite woman in

Matthew 15:21-28. Her daughter was suffering terribly from demon possession, and she sought Jesus' help. Initially, Jesus seemed to ignore her plea, then compared her situation to giving the children's bread to dogs. But she didn't waver. Her faith and persistence led Jesus to commend her great faith and heal her daughter. This story shows that even when it seems like God is silent or distant, maintaining faith and persistently seeking Him can lead to miracles.

So, how do we draw parallels between these stories and our lives? First, understand that persistence in faith involves a continuous dialogue with God, even when immediate answers aren't apparent. It's about clinging to the hope and assurance that He is listening and will respond in His time. When facing life's obstacles, keep knocking on God's door. This relentless pursuit not only strengthens your faith but also builds resilience.

Let's consider modern-day applications. Picture yourself in a difficult situation at work where opportunities seem scarce. Approach it with the same tenacity as the widow or the Canaanite woman. Start by:

- Reaffirming your faith daily, even when discouragement sets in.
- Surrounding yourself with supportive individuals who encourage your persistence.
- Reflecting on past instances where persistence paid off,

fueling your motivation.

Unwavering faith holds incredible power in overcoming obstacles. The story of Job is another profound illustration. Job lost everything—his wealth, children, and health—yet he remained faithful. His trust in God's wisdom never faltered, despite the extreme suffering. Today, many endure hardships such as job loss, illnesses, or betrayal. Maintaining faith like Job's helps navigate these trials with grace and fortitude.

Now, let's delve into how persistence in prayer and faith leads to breakthroughs. Persistent prayer is an ongoing conversation with God. It doesn't mean repetitive or monotonous requests; rather, it's about deepening your relationship with Him. Consider Daniel, who continued praying despite the decree outlawing worshiping any god other than King Darius. His steadfastness landed him in the lion's den, yet God delivered him unharmed. This demonstrates that consistency in prayer aligns our hearts with God's will, often resulting in divine intervention and protection.

What can you do to achieve this sort of breakthrough?

- Begin each day with a simple prayer, expressing your trust and reliance on God.
- Take moments throughout your day to pause, breathe, and reconnect with God through quick prayers.
- Before bed, reflect on your day and express gratitude,

solidifying your faith journey.

Through these practices, you'll cultivate a persistent prayer life that keeps you anchored during life's storms. Thus, persistence in faith doesn't just address immediate problems; it molds you into a resilient individual capable of weathering prolonged adversities.

In conclusion, let the key takeaways from these Biblical examples inspire you. Persistence in faith means never giving up on God because He never gives up on you. When faced with challenges, remember the widow who wouldn't quit and the Canaanite woman who pushed past barriers. Emulate Job's unwavering faith amid suffering and Daniel's steadfast prayers amidst danger. Through persistent prayer and undying faith, you'll find strength and victory in your own life's challenges.

Practical strategies for developing spiritual endurance in times of difficulty.

Developing a Persistent Prayer Life

Maintaining consistency and fervency in prayer can seem daunting. But it's essential not only for our spiritual growth but also for building resilience. Here are some steps to help you develop a persistent prayer life:

- Schedule it: Make prayer a priority by setting aside specific times each day to engage with God. Treat these moments as important appointments.

- Create a prayer list: Jot down the people, issues, and areas of your life you want to lift up in prayer. This helps maintain focus and track answered prayers.

- Ask for God's help: Seek His assistance to be consistent, knowing that He understands your challenges and wants to support you.

Leaning on God for Strength and Resilience

Life is full of ups and downs, and it's crucial to lean on God for strength and resilience. Start by acknowledging your dependency on Him. Recognize that true strength comes from surrendering your struggles to God and tapping into His infinite power. When feeling overwhelmed, take a moment to pause and ask for His guidance and strength. Remember, His grace is sufficient, and He promises never to leave us or forsake us.

Offering Methods to Stay Connected to God Through Prayer and Meditation Staying connected to God requires deliberate effort. Here are a few methods to maintain that connection:

- Engage in daily prayer: Make it a habit to converse with God regularly, sharing your thoughts, fears, and praises.

- Meditate on scripture: Spend time reflecting on Bible verses that speak to your heart. This practice helps keep God's word fresh in your mind.

- Practice gratitude: Regularly thank God for His blessings. Gratitude shifts your focus from problems to His goodness.

Encouraging Readers to Trust in the Process Despite Setbacks

Setbacks are inevitable, but trusting in the process is key to cultivating persistence and resilience through faith. It's easy to get disheartened when things don't go as planned, but remember that growth often occurs during challenging times. Trust that God has a plan for you, even if it's not immediately apparent. Embrace setbacks as opportunities to grow closer to Him, and let them strengthen your reliance on His wisdom and timing.

Addressing the challenges of setbacks and disappointments in the journey of faith.

Navigating disappointments is something we all face, but learning to reframe them as opportunities for growth can truly change our perspective. When you encounter a setback, it's essential to see it not as a dead end but as a detour guiding you toward a better path.

Here is what you can do to navigate disappointments:

- Reflect on the situation and identify what went wrong. This isn't about blaming yourself or others but about understanding the circumstances.
- Consider what you could have done differently. Think of

alternative actions or decisions that might lead to a better outcome next time.

- Focus on the positive aspects. Even with disappointments, there are often elements that go well. Acknowledge these successes, no matter how small.

- Use this experience to grow. Every disappointment carries a lesson. Embrace the learning opportunity and use it to improve your future endeavors.

Providing tools for resilience and perseverance in the face of adversity is crucial. Resilience doesn't mean avoiding hardships but rather recovering from them stronger than before. Here's how you can build resilience:

- Cultivate a positive mindset. Believe in your ability to overcome obstacles and view challenges as fleeting phases.

- Develop strong relationships. Surround yourself with supportive friends and family who can offer encouragement and advice during tough times.

- Set realistic goals. Break down larger tasks into smaller, manageable steps to maintain progress without feeling overwhelmed.

- Practice self-care. Take care of your physical and mental health through exercise, meditation, and hobbies that rejuvenate you.

Encouraging readers to find lessons and silver linings in challenging situations is vital. When faced with difficulties, looking for the positives can shift your focus from what's lost to what can be gained.

Here's how to discover silver linings:

- Reassess your goals and values. Difficulties often prompt us to reflect on what truly matters, helping us realign our priorities.
- Recognize personal growth. Adversity can foster resilience, empathy, and inner strength, contributing to your overall character development.
- Find gratitude. Identify at least one thing you're thankful for each day, even during tough times. Gratitude can lighten your outlook and provide hope.
- Inspire others. Your journey through challenges can serve as motivation for those around you, demonstrating that it's possible to emerge stronger after adversity.

Emphasizing the importance of trusting God's plan despite setbacks is easier said than done. But having faith that there's a greater purpose can provide comfort and guidance when things don't go as planned. Trusting God means believing that He sees the bigger picture, even when we can't. It means holding onto hope and continuing to pray, knowing that every hardship brings us closer to

His ultimate plan for us.

Key takeaways from this chapter are fundamental. Developing a mindset of resilience and hope enables you to look at disappointments not as failures but as stepping stones. By reflecting on our experiences, leaning on supportive relationships, practicing self-care, setting realistic goals, and maintaining a positive mindset, we can persevere through adversity. Finding lessons and silver linings in every challenge helps us grow and appreciate the journey, even when it's tough. And above all, trusting God's plan provides an anchor of faith that keeps us steady, regardless of life's storms.

Sharing personal reflections on persistent faith.

Looking back on the moments of persistent faith in my life, I can see how deeply these experiences have shaped me. One story that stands out is when I was fresh out of college and facing a tough job market. The uncertainty was nerve-wracking, but I remember a moment sitting quietly one night, feeling overwhelmed by the weight of it all. In that stillness, I prayed, pouring out my fears and worries. It felt like a release, and from that point, I began to experience a quiet strength within.

My journey wasn't without its hurdles. Rejections came in waves, each one more disheartening than the last. But every evening, I would take a moment to reconnect with my faith. This regular act of faith became a source of resilience and persistence.

Slowly, things began to shift. I got an interview for a position that seemed tailor-made for me. It wasn't just about landing a job; it was about recognizing that through faith, perseverance had brought me to a place where I felt more grounded and prepared for whatever lay ahead.

Another profound testimony comes from my mind of a friend. She faced the unimaginable—a serious illness that threatened her life. She approached her battle with a blend of determination and unwavering faith. Her days were filled with treatments and hospital visits, yet she made sure to prioritize her spiritual health. She once, shared how visualizing herself healed, while fervently praying gave her the courage to face each day. While the road was arduous, her faith provided the necessary stamina.

This recovery was slow, but each small victory, like being able to walk a few steps unaided, felt monumental. She often credited her progress to not just medical treatment but to the powerful combination of prayer and persistence. These small measures of improvement illustrated the power of faith in her personal journey.

Then there's Jake, whose childhood was marked by instability and loss. He grew up in a neighborhood where opportunities were scarce and adversity plentiful. Despite these challenges, Jake found solace and direction in his faith community.

He speaks often about the mentors who invested time in him, showing how faith in action can be transformative. Jake's story is a testament to how faith can fuel persistence even in the most challenging circumstances.

As he navigated high school and later college, his persistence bore fruit. Today, Jake works as a community organizer, helping others find their path through similar hardships. His story highlights how enduring faith can inspire and uplift not just oneself but entire communities.

Each of these stories offers a glimpse into the extraordinary power of faith and persistence. They remind us that success isn't always immediate, and goals aren't always reached overnight. Persistence, bolstered by faith, propels us forward, turning obstacles into growth opportunities.

From my own life to my friend's battle against illness and Jake's rise above hardship, we see that faith isn't passive. It's active and dynamic, something that requires our continual engagement. This engagement builds resilience. We find strength in knowing we are supported by a greater force, one that guides us through even the darkest times.

For readers, these real-life examples serve as powerful motivators. When faced with difficulties, remembering these testimonies can foster a sense of connection and inspiration. It's important to take time to reflect on your own experiences of faith and persistence. Reflect on those moments where you felt a surge of inner strength or clarity. Recognize that these instances aren't coincidences but testaments to the power of faith working in your life.

Faith and persistence together create a blueprint for navigating life's trials. They teach us to remain steadfast, reminding us that every step forward, no matter how small, is part of a larger, divine plan. Therefore, when you're standing at the crossroads of doubt and hope, lean into your faith. Let it guide you, fortify you, and remind you that, like Sarah, Jake, and myself, you too can overcome and thrive.

Through our personal testimonies and those shared by others, we draw strength and motivation. These narratives help us see the beauty in persistence and the transformative power of unwavering faith. Keep reflecting on these stories. Let them be a bedrock for your journey, encouraging you to persist, believe, and witness the incredible changes faith can bring into your life.

Key Takeaways.

In this chapter, we've delved into how persistence and resilience can be cultivated through faith by reflecting on inspiring Biblical examples. From the persistent widow in Luke to the Canaanite woman in Matthew, these stories highlight the power of unwavering faith and persistent prayer. Whether it's facing modern-day challenges like career hurdles or personal conflicts, their lessons remain timeless.

We also discussed practical ways to develop a consistent prayer life and lean on God for strength and resilience. Setting regular prayer times, creating prayer lists, and expressing gratitude are simple yet effective strategies to stay connected with God. Leaning on Him during tough times helps us build spiritual endurance and navigate life's ups and downs with grace.

Navigating setbacks and disappointments is part of everyone's journey. Reflecting on what went wrong, considering alternative actions, and focusing on the positives can transform setbacks into valuable learning experiences. Resilience means bouncing back from hardships stronger than before, not avoiding them altogether. Cultivating a positive mindset, building strong relationships, setting realistic goals, and practicing self-care all contribute to developing perseverance.

Personal testimonies highlight the transformative power of faith and persistence. My own job search journey, My friend's battle with illness, and Jake's rise above childhood adversity show that success often follows prolonged efforts and unwavering faith. These real-life examples serve as powerful motivators, reminding us that faith isn't passive but active and dynamic.

The key takeaway here is simple: persistence in faith means never giving up on God because He never gives up on you. When faced with challenges, think of the widow who wouldn't quit, the Canaanite woman who pushed past barriers, and Job's unwavering faith. Remember Daniel's steadfast prayers and trust that your persistent prayer will anchor you through life's storms.

As you reflect on your own experiences of faith, let these narratives inspire and encourage you. Keep persisting, keep believing, and witness the incredible changes faith can bring into your life. The journey might be tough, but with faith and persistence, you'll find strength and victory in your challenges. Let your faith guide and fortify you, knowing that each step forward is part of a larger, divine plan.

References

Dr. Schubiner - Understanding and Overcoming Fear. TMS Forum (The Mind body Syndrome). (n.d.). https://www.tmswiki.org. / forum/threads/ understanding-and-overcoming-fear.182/.

Guber, P. (2011, February). *Using Stories to Overcome Fear. Harvard Business Review.* https:// hbr.org/2011/02/using-stories-to-overcome-fear.

Ingram, C. (2021, September). *4 Clear Steps To Applying The Wisdom Of God To Our Lives. Living on the Edge.* https://livingontheedge.org/ 2021/09/06/4-steps-to-applying-wisdom-of-god/.

*Fruits Of The Beatitudes | Premise | Concept

'Refinement'. * (n.d.). https://fruitsof thebeatitudes.org/concept-refinement/.

How To Embrace and Overcome Adversity proverbs31. org. (n.d.).https://proverbs31.org/read/ devotions/full-post/2023/05/02/how-to-embraceand-overcome-adversity.

Johnson, E. (n.d.). *More Than Conquerors through Him That Loved Us. www.churchofjesuschrist.org.* https://www.churcho fjesuschrist.org/study/generalconference/2011/04/more-than-conquerorsthrough-him-that-loved-us?lang=eng.

THE PATIENCE OF JOSEPH. pacificcog.org. (n.d.). https://pacificcog.org/transcript/063012RR.html.

Tomlinson, P. (2024, January). *Journey to Healing: Embracing the Transformative Power of Jesus - Part 2. Timothy Tomlinson.* https://www.timothytomlinson.org/single-post/journey-tohealing-embracing-the-transformative-power-ofjesus-part-2.

University, C. (2024). *Unraveling the Depths of Divine Grace CCU Online. Ccu.edu.* https://www.ccu.edu/blogs/cags/category/devotionals/ unraveling-the-depths-of-divine-grace/.

Apostles, E. (n.d.). *Ask in Faith. www.churchofjesuschrist. org.* https://www.churchofjesuschrist.org/study/generalconference/2008/04/ask-in-faith?lang=eng.

Foundations for Prayer Toward the Global Purpose of God. Desiring God. (2000, September). https:/ www.desiringgod.org / messages/foundations-forprayer-toward-the-global-purpose-of-god.

Get Through Anything: Here's How to Build a Sure Foundation — Faith Chapel. Faith Chapel Assembly of God Pleasanton. (n.d.). https://agfaithchapel.org/ sermons-messages/get-through-anything-heres-howto-build-a-sure-foundation.

135

Hogan, S. (2023, June). *The Importance of Church as a Community. GCU.* https://www.gcu.edu/blog/ theology-ministry/importance-church-community.

Taylor, K. (2020, September). *20 Bible verses for faith-motivated advocacy. World Vision Advocacy.* https://worldvisionadvocacy.org/2020/09/22/20bible-verses-for-faith-motivated-advocacy/.

The Importance of Church Community. CU Online. (2020, August). https://online.campbellsville.edu/ ministry/importance-of-church-community/.

Willis, A. (2016, September). *How To Build A Strong Faith Foundation In Our Kids' Lives. They Call Me Blessed.* https://www.theycallmeblessed.org/strongfaith-foundation/.

"Allen, J. (2022, August). Five Steps to Renewing *Your Mind. Open the Bible.* https://openthebible.org/article/five-steps-to-renewingyour-mind/.

Here's how I found freedom from fear. ActiveChristianity. (2020, May). https://activechristianity.org/heres-how-i-found-freedomfrom-fear.

Ingram, C. (2022, March). *5 Practical Steps to Renew Your Mind and Replace Negative Thoughts. Living on the Edge.* https://livingontheedge.org/ 2022/03/28/5-steps-to-renew-your-mind/.

Apostles, E. (n.d.). *Personal Peace in Challenging Times.* *www.churchofjesuschrist.org.* https://www.churchofjesuschrist.org/study/generalconference/2021/10/46cook?lang=eng.

Finding Peace in the Midst of Chaos. proverbs31.org. (n.d.). https://proverbs31.org/read/devotions/fullpost/2019/09/16/finding-peace-in-the-midst-ofchaos.

Grace, S. (2020, September). *7 Christian Mindfulness Exercises to See God in Daily Life. Calming Grace.* https://www.stewardshipoflife.org/2020/12/ christian-mindfulness-exercises-to-see-god-in-dailylife/.

Savoring the Peace of Jesus in a Chaotic World. proverbs31.org. (n.d.). https://proverbs31.org/read/ devotions/full-post/2024/03/04/savoring-thepeace-of-jesus-in-a-chaotic-world.

*The Power Of Gratitude | Full Strength Network. * (n.d.). https://fullstrength.org/the-power-ofgratitude/.

University, C. (2024). *Gratitude: A Journey of Faith and Transformation | CCU Online. Ccu.edu.* https://www.ccu.edu/blogs/cags/category/devotionals/ gratitude-a-journey-of-faith-and-transformation/.

*[Jubilee columns] Unfolding Praise: 7. The Power of Praise in Personal and Corporate Spiritual Growth – jubileeschool.org. * (n.d.). https://jubileeschool.org/ jubilee-columns-unfolding-praise-7-the-power-ofpraise-in-personal-and-corporate-spiritual-growth/.

4 Biblical Keys to Breakthrough Prayer that Works | King Jesus Ministry. 4 Biblical Keys to Breakthrough Prayer that Works | King Jesus Ministry. (n.d.). https://www.kingjesus.org/blog/news/4-biblicalkeys-to-breakthrough-prayer-that-works.

God Answers Hannah's Prayer. Mission Bible Class. (2011, December). https://missionbibleclass.org/oldtestament/part2/judges-and-ruth/god-answershannahs-prayer/.

How To Build Godly Character. The Church of God International. (n.d.). https://www.cgi.org/how-tobuild-godly-character.

Miracles and Answered Prayers. Nauvoo Neighbor. (2022, February).https://nauvooneighbor.org/latterday-saint-witness-testimony/miracles-andanswered-prayers/.

True Prayers Answered Stories Archives.

Guideposts. (n.d.). https://guideposts.org/prayer/ true-stories-of-answered-prayer/.

Waiting for Breakthrough. proverbs31.org. (n.d.).

https://proverbs31.org/read/devotions/full-post/ 2018/06/19/waiting-for-breakthrough.

What is the importance and value of group prayer?

GotQuestions.org. (n.d.). https:// www.gotquestions.org/group-prayer.html.

wisitech. (2022, February). 10 Powerful Miracle Prayers for

Financial Help from God. *The Salvation Garden*. https://www.thesalvationgarden.org/10powerful-miracle-prayers-for-financial-help-fromgod/.

GotQuestions.org Testimonials. GotQuestions.org. (n.d.). https://www.gotquestions.org/ testimonials.html.

How can I increase my spiritual discernment?.

GotQuestions.org. (n.d.). https://www.gotquestions.org/spiritual-discernment.html.

How to Develop Your Spiritual Discernment.

Ligonier Ministries. (n.d.). https://www.ligonier.org/learn/articles/how-develop-your-spiritualdiscernment.

Robinson, M. (2018, June). *How to Use Your Spiritual Authority in Any Situation. KCM Blog.*

https://blog.kcm.org/use-spiritual-authoritysituation/.

Spiritual Authority 101: What It Is and Why It Matters [Video]. Novo. (n.d.). https://novo.org/ discipleship-blog/spiritual-authority-101-what-it-isand-why-it-matters-video.

True Stories of Faith in God: God Saved My Daughter From Death | GOSPEL OF THE DESCENT OF THE KINGDOM. www.holyspiritspeaks.org. (n.d.). https://www.holyspiritspeaks.org/testimonies/true-stories-of-faith-in-God/.

*4 Reasons Accountability Is Invaluable in the Christian Life - Jesus Film Project. * (2021, October).

https://www.jesusfilm.org/blog/accountabilityinvaluable-christian-life/.

Community - Acts 2:42-47. Redeemer Anglican Church. (2020, March). https://redeemerrva.org/tee-feyrer-blogpage/2020/3/communityacts-242-47.

Cultivating Attentiveness to God's Presence. C.S. Lewis Institute. (n.d.). https:// www.cslewisinstitute.org/resources/cultivatingattentiveness-to-gods-presence/.

Five things that we can learn from the early Church. www.elim.org.uk. (n.d.). https://elim.org/Articles/ 525131/Five_things_that.aspx.

Growing Through Small Groups. Discipleship Ministries. (n.d.). https://www.umcdiscipleship.org/ resources/growing-through-small-groups.

Understanding and Developing Christian Accountability. Churchleadership.org. (2024).

http://www.churchleadership.org/apps/articles/default.asp?articleid=42506.

Wellons, A. (2019, November). *Relying on God Isn't a Mind Game. The Gospel Coalition.* https:// www.thegospelcoalition.org /article/relying-god-isntmind-game/.

www.ingramcontent.com/pod-product-compliance
Lightning Source LLC
Chambersburg PA
CBHW051527120626
46551CB00012B/1107